Our Side of the River
by Sis Laraux

A biography of growing up and living in Alaska on
our side of the Kuskokwim River in the village of Old Akiak.

ISBN 0-9644809-0-5

Library of Congress Catalog Card Number: 94-62116

Published by Publication Consultants
P.O. Box 443, Palmer, Alaska 99645

RECOGNITION

My teacher, Kathy Turner, an instructor at Mat/Su College, who encouraged me to publicize my stories and photo's, my sisters and Uncle Elias, who recalled stories and sent photographs, sister Bess for copy writing and corrections, friend, Gyda Fredericksen, for photos, and daughter Rene´e and husband, Jim, for helping prepare this manuscript.

DEDICATION

To my sisters and brother, and their families, Brother Butch's wife and family, close friends and relatives who are left from our days at Akiak, Alaska. Grandchildren and Great-grandchildren and especially to my loving children, who I fondly refer to as "My little Ball of Yarn."

Sis Laraux—Eskimo name "Ugoovak"

Ana Venes—Grandma Annun—Village midwife.

Nome

Anvik   Fairbanks

McGrath

Holy Cross

Bering Sea

Akiak Aniak
Nyac
Bethel   Alaska Range   Wasilla

Anchorage

Platinum   Valdez

Kuskokwim Bay

Klondike
Yukon Territory

Dawson

9

Index

INTRODUCTION

I share with you the story of my life in the remote village of Akiak, located on the Kuskokwim River in Western Alaska. Akiak is about 40 miles up river, west, from Bethel and approximately 400 miles west of Anchorage.

The main village of Akiak, referred to by the BIA (Bureau of Indian Affairs), is on one side of the river and the other side, and all who lived there, are referred to as "Our Side of the River."

My story is a personal and treasured story of how I was born and raised in this remote Eskimo village, recalling the first settlers, their families, and the many nationalities who settled in Akiak, we came to know them all. Our life in Akiak was hard, but we worked together as a large family overcoming tragedies and obstacles but still arranging fun times and happiness. There were no strangers among us.

Fond memories will always mingle in our present day with those on "Our Side of the River."

Akiak

The village of Akiak is situated on both the east and west side of the Kuskokwim River, 40 miles northwest of Bethel. The Eskimo reservation, located on the east side, was governed by the Bureau of Indian Affairs. It included a BIA school and also the first BIA hospital in the area, and that was where I was born.

In 1933, the hospital was torn down and rebuilt in Bethel, 40 miles north, the metropolis of the coastal area. The BIA side of the Kuskokwim had a large Eskimo settlement.

An Eskimo, and rustic character named Joe Williams, owned a trading post on the BIA side. It was considered a general store and sold groceries, dry goods, and various necessities. An adjoining room housed a pool table and also doubled as a silent theater. He owned a sawmill too. Buildings on the BIA side included government housing for hospital and teacher staff and the Moravian church with their parsonages.

The first missionaries on the river came from Bethel, Pennsylvania. That is how Bethel Alaska got its name.

On the west side, our side of the river at Akiak, there were 75 to 100 inhabitants during the winter months and less than half that during the summer. The residents were mostly miners who wintered there but went back to other jobs during the summer. The older teenagers left for summer jobs, too, usually finding work at Bethel or on sternwheelers or freight barges, or in the New York Alaska Corporation's gold mines (Nyac village, founded in 1915, was named after this mining company), platinum mines, or at the Bristol Bay canneries.

In the early 1900's Laplanders of the Saami tribe, and their families, were sent from northern Norway to Alaska with their own reindeer herds. This was a government venture to encourage reindeering in Alaska. Also, the Laplanders came to train the Eskimos how to manage and care for the reindeer. Four herds were placed in different areas of Alaska: Nome, Unalakleet, Bristol Bay, and Akiak, on our side of the river. The Laplanders built their homes and settled down with their families. Among them were the four Sara brothers, Peter, Michael, Clement, and Morton, Per Spein, Ole Polk, and Per Ante.

I was born April 8, 1927 at the government hospital, on the other side of the river. About 1933 the hospital was torn down and a new one built in Bethel. The Moravian Church is at the left.

My grandfather, Joseph Venes, built a couple of bunk houses for the miners in the early 1900's. The miners came in late fall to winter over until spring . I fondly remember John Hitz, Red Bean, Jack O'Keefe, Jim Downey, Big Hans, Little Hans, Scotty Auld (the photographer), Jerry Frankie, Ed McCann, Neil Corrigal, Frank McDougal, Scotty Morrison, and Earl Forrest. It always delighted us kids because when they'd arrive from the mines, they'd take us to the store for sweets—buying us pop and candy—a special treat back then.

Among our regular inhabitants were two Norwegian brothers, Alfred and Ole Anderson and their families. The Alfred Anderson family had two sons, Raymond and Melvin. The Ole Anderson's had a son, Rolf, and a daughter, Dorothy, another daughter Marguerite, had died at an early age, Alfred and Ole had a half brother named Jens Kvamme, who later moved to Akiak from Aniak. Aniak is about 100 miles above Akiak, west, on the Kuskokwim River. Jens had married the Sara daughter and they had children named Albert, James, and Berntina. Two older daughters were grown, married and lived elsewhere. The Anderson brothers owned a gold mine at Canyon Creek. They would go up in early spring to work the mine and back to Akiak and their families for the winter.

Minnie Kawagley who was married to Ben, an Eskimo from the other side of the river, got a divorce. She moved over to our side with her family: Adam, Catherine, Alice, and Elsie They lived on the outskirts of our village. She was a hard working lady—supporting her children—and later had two more children, Jack and Ethel.

Grandma Mary Smith, a heavy-set, strong, Thlinget Indian woman from Haines, Alaska, moved to Akiak with her son Patrick. She had two grown sons Dudley and Clarence, both married with young families . They stayed at the New York Alaska gold mine, Nyac as we called it.

My father, Louis Joseph Arthur L'Heureux, shortened his name to Laraux. He met my mother, Lena Venes, and married her on Thanksgiving Day in November 1922. He then built the large comfortable log home on the left and settled in Akiak. The Venes home and bunkhouse is on the right.

When children were school age, the parents could send one or two down to Grandma Smith at Akiak to spend the winter and attend school. Then, there were no schools at Nyac.

Joe Chaney, Sr., a Frenchman and miner, who came to Alaska during the Dawson gold rush, settled at Akiak and mined at Nyac also. He built a nice log cabin and had five sons: William, Fred, Amedee (Middy), Joe Jr, and George.

Joe Sr. was divorced and had custody of his sons. He was forced to send his boys to Holy Cross Mission for proper care and schooling. Holy Cross Mission was a Catholic boarding school on the Yukon River, at the village of Holy Cross, After the boys were grown and of work age, he brought them home to Akiak.

The Akiak residents were an interesting collection of people. We children were trained to call the older people formally as Mr. and Mrs.

There was such a variety of nationalities: French Norwegian, Irish, Scottish, Polish, Swedes, and Laplanders.

The Ole and Alfred Anderson homes in Akiak

Gold miners in general are known to be a rowdy bunch, so it is amazing there was no violence or crime. With such a mixture of different races, speaking different dialects, it's no wonder we wound up with such

The Laraux home in Akiak where I grew up.

pronounced accents.

One interesting note worth mentioning; there were no African black people around. The first one I saw was when I was 17 years old. I had moved up to Fairbanks to live with my married sister, Hanna, while working and attending high school up there. *Sis*

My Father

My father, Louis Joseph Arthur L'Heureux, came to Alaska during the 1898 Klondike gold rush stampede at Dawson. He actually walked over Chilkoot Pass to get there. He left his home in St. Marie, Quebec at the age of 16. He was one of 12 children. Records show his first name to be Louis but everyone called him Arthur. After he came to Alaska, he shortened his name to Laraux. Around the age of 18, he took one last trip home to Quebec to visit with his ailing mother, Philomena.

After the Dawson stampede, several miners rafted down the Yukon River to another gold rush at Iditarod and Flat. In the early 1900s when the gold fever dwindled, my father and his mining partner, Wilfred Reno, came down the Kuskokwim River. Reno was also a French Canadian. They wound up in Akiak. Arthur met my mother, Lena Venes, and married her on Thanksgiving Day in November 1922. He then built a large comfortable log home and settled in Akiak.

My father was one of the nicest men I've ever known. He was respected by the community as well as his family. He was gentle, patient, and helpful to all he came in contact with. We were never spanked but had to explain a lot if we had done wrong. His stern, cold stare gave us the message that we had done wrong. It made a lasting impression on us. Papa was congenial and had a smile for everyone. He smoked Rio-tan cigars and in later life changed to a pipe with rum flavored tobacco. It brings back memories whenever I smell someone smoking that brand. He had a strong French accent and cussed a lot but it was never vulgar. It was his way to converse.

My father didn't speak too much about his early days of mining around Dawson Creek or about the Iditarod stampede. Once in a while he'd share a few stories. Travel was very challenging with ferocious mosquitos to contend with in summer, especially while traveling from one gold bed to another. It was very hard work. The bears were plentiful, too. The miners had to travel in groups, hauling all their equipment in pack sacks on their backs. Walking through the meadows and high grass, whether there was a bear or not, they'd pound cooking pans together. This created a lot of noise to scare the bears away. To make sleds, or log rafts to get across streams, but with no decent tools to work with, was another hardship. The food selection was very limited too. Someone was elected daily to stop and build a fire, then cook some beans in a cast iron pot over the campfire. Beans that were left over would be frozen, in late fall they'd pry out a hunk of frozen beans and warm it in a frying pan. Sometimes someone was lucky enough to get wild game and a stew was made, if not, they relied on

Papa invested in a small sawmill, which came in handy not only for us, but our other village inhabitants as well. Above, Papa and Johnny Hitz operating the mill. My father was one of the nicest men I've ever known. He was respected by the community as well as his family. He was gentle, patient, and helpful to all he came in contact with. We were never spanked but had to explain a lot if we had done wrong. His stern, cold stare gave us the message that we had done wrong. It made a lasting impression on us. Papa was congenial and had a smile for everyone.

beans as their basic food. Anything warm was especially enjoyable. A sourdough pot was always kept mixed and was protected to keep it from freezing. Bread was not available and hot cakes, cooked over the campfire, was a good start for a hard days work. Sourdough hot cakes have since become a tradition in Alaska.

Other miners made a gold strike at Iditarod, word spread and a large log raft was built, referred to as a scow, and a bunch of miners rafted down the Yukon River to Iditarod country. It took many days to get there from

20

Dawson. Iditarod mining camp was quite well established—some large buildings, many miners and even a house of prostitution. The manager was a black lady named "Tootsie". The miners had great respect for her since she'd grubstake poor miners to get them started. After those miners hit pay dirt, they would repay their bill. There were always some that didn't strike it lucky, though. Tootsie Crosby lived in Alaska at Flat and Iditarod for 63 years and died at the Sitka Pioneer Home in 1960.

Papa was a successful miner. My mother had a lot of jewelry made with the Alaska gold he'd mined over the years. Mom's jewelry is now divided among us children. There was no welfare in those days but we never needed it. There were seven of us children and we always seem to have a few extra kids with us but, we were never hungry. Papa was a hard working man and kept the woodshed full. Papa eventually invested in a small sawmill, which came in handy not only for us but our other village

Papa, Mama, and Hanna in Bethel. My father, Louis Joseph Arthur L'Heureux, was one of 12 children. Everyone called him Arthur. After he came to Alaska, he shortened his name to Laraux.

inhabitants as well.

In the summer, Papa built a neck yolk to carry two five gallons of water up from the river for filling our water barrels. In the winter months he hauled barrels of water in the sled with the help of a few dogs. We had no running water and with all our laundry, cleaning, chores, cooking, and bathing we always needed a lot.

Papa also built an ice house; it was heavily insulated with sawdust and close to our house. He and the other men cut ice blocks from the river to store. We melted ice water in a crock and had a water scoop or dipper to drink from. We'd also collect rain water in the summer for drinking. If we ran out, we drank river water but it always had to be boiled for sanitary reasons. Everyone's roof was covered with sheet metal to catch the rain.

Papa did all the fishing while we were small. Then Amedee "Middy" Chaney decided to stay with us and he helped Papa with chores. Middy stayed with us for quite awhile; When my brothers were old enough they helped fish, too.

Papa went to work on the river boats. He was the engineer for Tony Sumi and his barging business. He remained with him until 1941 when Tony was sent off to a Japanese concentration camp on the west coast. Papa was then hired at Nyac gold mine, located in the hills above Akiak. Since he was gone during the spring and summer months, Middy remained with us to help at home. He came to be like one of the family.

Papa had his own workshop where he built dandy dog sleds and boats. When the neighbors needed something built or repaired he was always there to help. I can remember him repairing shoes for people. He had a shoe repair kit made of cast iron with different sizes of shoe

Papa holding me. Mama, Hanna, and Sonny. Papa, owned a blacksmith shop and made skates, horseshoes, and sled runners. He built various furniture pieces for our home; including cupboards, dressers, small tables, rocking chairs, and straight-back chairs, a baby crib, and high chair.

molds. Papa was kept pretty busy just repairing or mending people's torn shoes or replacing a heel and even fixing shoes to relieve Mrs. Alfreds

Anderson's bunions. Middy Chaney's youngest brother, George, had moved back from Holy Cross Mission. While there, George lost a leg in a sawmill accident. It seemed Papa was always fixing or repairing George's wooden leg so George could walk properly. George had moved in with Grandma's family.

In addition to his workshops, Papa, owned a blacksmith shop complete with anvil. He made skates, horseshoes, sled runners, and other items including wood heaters built out of 50 gallon drums. Besides iron work, he built various furniture pieces for our home; including cupboards, dressers, small tables, rocking chairs, and straight-back chairs. Also, a baby crib and high chair which were passed on down through our family. Some of these are still in use today.

There was always action in Akiak. Travelers were coming and going by boat and by dog team. Whenever anyone arrived, Papa always greeted them and invited them in for a warm meal or even just a cup of coffee and snack before they went on their way.

Willie Chaney and Sonny home on leave from the Service.

We had a dandy sourdough pot Papa made. It was hewed out of a large log, with the wood contents all scooped out, and sanded inside and out. It even had a lid. No one was able to tell it was handmade because it cooked so perfect. The sourdough pot was kept going almost daily in order to have good, tasty, sourdough hot cakes. We always saved enough starter mix, a fermented yeast mixture, for the next batch. I remember the homemade syrup we poured on those hot cakes, too. Even today I love hot cakes made with homemade syrup.

During the wild berry season, Papa would take a few days off from his job. He would come home to mend our fish nets or to catch up on needed chores. In those days, we had to weave our own nets and it was an art not everyone could master. Once the necessary chores were completed, Papa would take us kids berry picking. There were no salmonberries or blueberries at Akiak, so we'd have to go to tundra areas in the nearby low

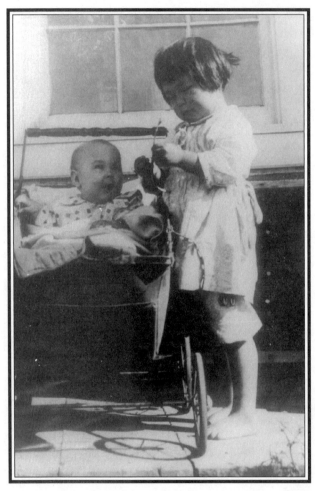

My sisters, Bessie and Cutie.

hills. We'd fix a lunch and take along lots of buckets or pails. We would head for a favorite slough up the river from Akiak called "Chownuk, " or below Akiak to the Kwethluk River. We had an inboard motor boat we called the "Took-took. "It was always so enjoyable to ride in our own boat chewing on a piece of dried smoked fish or else eating hardtack with a piece of Spam on top.

Berry picking was a family event. We'd even have berry picking contests. We knew Papa would win because he was left-handed and could pick with both hands. I have a daughter, Barbara, who has inherited his style of berry picking. Anyway, at the end of the day, we'd all climb back into our boat and head for home. Everyone was tired but we had all of our buckets full of berries, ready to clean and store away or eat. The salmonberries and blueberries were used in various ways, mainly for jams, jellies, pies, Eskimo ice cream (agootuk), or as a desert with sugar and cream.

24

As we were growing up, we were always trying to trace our father's side of the family. He lost track of his family while mining in Flat, due to losing all possessions and addresses in a bunk house fire where he resided. We would write letters that inevitably came back. By chance, we eventually located a few relatives, thanks to Dr. Langsom at the BIA hospital in Bethel. He received a letter of inquiry and passed along the information to us. This was in the mid 1940s and I was in my teens then.

The first personal letter we received from our distant relatives was written in French. Papa had forgotten how to read French so Father Menager, our traveling Jesuit Priest, translated the letter for us. It was hard to believe we had finally located Papa's relatives. There was so much joy and jubilation among our family, along with our neighbors and friends. We learned that Papa's family was scattered throughout Canada and Maine. Word quickly spread among his lost siblings that their brother had been located in Akiak, Alaska. Then the letters started. Our family in Alaska all wished Papa would go visit in St. Marie, situated about 40-50

The Chaneys: Willie, Middie, Joe, Fred, and George. While at Holy Cross Mission, George lost a leg in a sawmill accident . It seemed Papa was always fixing or repairing George's wooden leg so George could walk properly.

miles south of Quebec city. He didn't want to go however; I think mainly because of his age, distance, and expense involved.

Our sister, Bess, while working for Alaska Airlines, traveled extensively one year and met relatives in Edmonton, Canada; New Westminister, British Columbia, Auburn, Maine, and then St. Marie, Canada. Uncle

Emel was the translator in Quebec province, since very few kin spoke English then. Language was no barrier and she was treated royally by all. Several of Papa's brothers and sisters were still alive. Our brother "Butch" was also fortunate enough later to pay a visit to Uncle Antonio, who was then Papa's last living brother. Butch met several other relatives in Maine since some of Papa's sisters migrated and settled there, too. He had an enjoyable visit.

Our parents adopted a 7 month boy named Charles.

After Papa passed away, one of our Maine cousins, Pat Masson, and husband Larry, came to Alaska to visit. We had a great get-to-gether and exchanged numerous stories and pictures. We still keep in touch with Patsy, various other cousins, and kin.

A Canadian schoolteacher who was fluent in English was kind enough to write letters for our French Canadian relatives. For several years she did this favor for our kin; apparently she is not there any longer. We still get letters written in French once in awhile, usually at Christmas, and have to locate an interpreter. *Sis*

26

My Mother

My mother, Lena (Eskimo name, Oogugula), was born in the village of Atmautlauk about 20 miles below Bethel, close to Nunapitchuk, on the Johnson River. My grandmother Anna, (we always called her Annun) was married before she married Grandpa Joseph, and had two daughters; my mother, Lena, and Bessie. Grandmother, Anna, moved to Akiak to be near the hospital, where she could get needed medicines. Here she met and married Joseph Venes, a Norwegian from Norway. He was an excellent carpenter, miner and boat builder. Later when Mama was older she met my Papa and they married Thanksgiving Day, November 1922. In turn, a few years later, Papa's mining partner,

Mama was the hunter of the family. She took ptarmigan and rabbit snares and a 20-gauge shotgun or a .22 rifle and always came home with game in her sled.

Wilfred Reno, married Mama's sister, Aunt Bessie.

There was seven of us children born to Mama and Papa. Our names were Hanna, Arthur Jr. "Sonny," Rosanna "Sis" (myself), Alfred "Butch," Bessie, Lena "Cutie," and Emel the youngest. Emel sadly died when he was 4 during an epidemic. Ruby Reno, our cousin, came to live with us after her mother died, so we acquired another sister. Later our parents adopted a 7 month boy named Charles, who was Ruby's half-brother.

Much like Papa, Mama was a most capable person. She was always making us clothes from old clothes, she made wonderfully warm coats and jackets. She also made pretty dresses from bolt goods. Mom owned a Singer treadle machine which still exists today. She also made us fur clothing. She did a lot of knitting: socks, sweaters, caps, scarves, mittens, and gloves. She baked a dozen loaves of bread a week along with oven rolls. The bread seemed especially delicious when we came home hungry from school. She was an amazing woman; such a hard working care-giver and provider.

Our family consisted of Mama and Papa, Hanna, Sis, Sonny, Bessie, Lena, Butch, and Emel the youngest.

Although Papa was the main provider, it was Mama who was the hunter of the family. I can't remember her once coming home without game. She'd hitch up two or three dogs to a small sled in the winter, dress in her hunting parkie and wolf mukluks that came up to her hips, and up the river she'd go. She took ptarmigan and rabbit snares and a 20-gauge shotgun or a .22 rifle. She always came home with game in her sled. In the early spring and fall, she'd go bird hunting for ducks and geese with her pack sack on her back. She was always an accurate shot. In turn, Mama cleaned all the game until we were old enough to help. She even had a canoe in which she would go muskrat hunting during the summer.

I remember when we girls had to clean the birds she'd bring us in early spring. Birds were out of season then, so we had to sit in the deep woods plucking feathers. We were always on the lookout for airplanes possibly bringing the game warden, but we never were caught.

One day my sister, Hanna, and I decided to go hunting. I had a single

28

shot .22 rifle and Hanna sported a 20-gauge shotgun. We were sneaking up on some ducks and geese, she ahead of me. All of a sudden my gun went

Hanna, Bessie, Papa, Cutie, Sonny, Mama, Sis, and Ruby.

off, right between her feet. Of course it scared us and the birds too. We

went home and decided it was best not to say a word. We knew we would get a good bawling out and be lectured on gun safety. We feared Mamma would never let us go hunting again, if she heard about the near miss.

One day our brother, Sonny, came home from hunting. While putting his gun up on the gun rack, off it went blasting at the ceiling. That was a big scare. He said he'd just unloaded it before he came in the house. Then Hanna and I told our story about our near miss while on a duck hunt. We still got a big lecture from Papa and Mama about gun safety.

Charlie and the dog, Prince.

It made me feel better that I wasn't the only careless one, though. *Sis*

29

Grandparents

My grandparents, Annun and Grandpa Joseph, lived right next door to us. There was a worn pathway between our two houses and if you couldn't find one of the kids at our house, you'd find them next door. Our grandparents had three children: Nora, Joseph Jr., and Elias. They were our age so we didn't use "Uncle" or "Aunt" when addressing them. Grandpa Joe Venes was a skilled carpenter. He was always building stores and homes for people at Bethel or Akiak. He was a good fisherman, too. He taught us exactly how to row, take care of a boat, how to fish, and take care of our catch. He made and repaired fish nets.

The only thorough spanking I ever got was from grandpa Venes. I can vividly remember it to this day. One fall day the potatoes were dug and spread out in the sun to dry before storing. Elias and I were outside playing and we spotted the potatoes. We decided to skate on the fresh potatoes as the skins are always slippery when they are freshly dug from the garden. We were having a great time when all of a sudden came a big rapping at the window. Out stormed Grandpa Venes with his hardwood stick. He caught us both and we really got a stern paddling. We never ever did that again!

Grandma Anna Venes was called "Annun," an Eskimo word meaning "your mother." She was born in the early spring, in a skin boat traveling from Nelson Island, on the Bering Sea, to the mainland. Since she didn't know her age, and her birth date was not recorded, her age was difficult to determine. There was one thing I have always treasured about "Annun," she made the best yeast donuts. We all knew when she was making them and we'd gather at her home after playing games, and enjoy the delicious donuts. She always made a dishpan full so there would be plenty for everyone.

There were always a lot of boys around Grandma's house besides Joe and Elias. Of course Wilfred Reno, our cousin, lived there and George Chaney was there frequently. Sometimes, whenever anyone got out of hand, she'd try to get a hold of them but couldn't because they moved too fast. Well, Grandpa made a broom stick with a hook at the end and her

The grandmas: Hall, Smeaton, Laraux, Linstrom, Jacobson, Freda Jacobson, and child, Hilda.

problem was solved. When they'd try to run away, grandma would grab the broom hook and catch them by their suspenders. That stopped them in a hurry.

Annun had a special, welcoming ceremony she'd perform on a new born baby, who came into the family. Taking the baby into her arms, holding it close for a while, she would then place it on her knee, talking silently to the baby in Eskimo, then moistening her finger into her mouth would make the sign of the cross on the baby's forehead. It was a special blessing for good luck and happiness for the newborn coming into this world.

Around 1933, the hospital was torn down and a new one built in Bethel. The BIA decided it would be the best place to serve the area, including the coastal villages. Grandma helped Mom with her last baby deliveries including Bessie, "Cutie," and Emel, because the hospital was further away. We'd be sent out of the house to play or visit and when we came home, there was a new baby to welcome. I recall it being an exciting experience to see a new baby. What a miracle it seemed to be.

Around 1935, Uncle Reno decided to get married again and he brought home a new bride. She was Oscar Samuelson's youngest daughter named Olga. They called her "Babe." Reno and Babe had two children named Ferdinand and Catherine, who both died at an early age. Ann Marie and Charles were born later. Olga had a daughter of her own named Augusta, prior to her marriage to Uncle Reno. She was my age so we had another friend.

Ruby and I would go with their family to visit Oscar Samuelson and his wife at their store in Oscarville, below Bethel. We enjoyed that. It was the first time I'd experienced taking a steam bath. Augusta's grandmother Samuelson had her own steam bath. What a refreshing feeling the warmth of a steam bath offers.

Uncle Reno brought the first gas-run washing machine to Akiak. It was so exciting and all of the women at Akiak were envious. Everyone had to have one then. It was such a great improvement over the washboards, which had been used until then. Next, came the gas irons and they did a much better job on the clothing, compared to the sad iron.

One day Olga was using her new washing machine and hanging her clothes outside on the line. She was busy running indoors and out, wearing a fancy squirrel skin parkie. Bending too close to the wringer, she got her wolf ruff stuck in it. The wringer tore the ruff completely off. She had long hair and it was getting caught, too. The turnoff switch was on the other side where she couldn't reach it. Luckily, someone came in while she was screaming. It was so fortunate someone came to her rescue. I had visions of what could have happened if someone didn't come in the door.

Charles was a baby of 7 months when his father, Uncle Reno, passed away. It was the agreement that my folks take and raise him. He took the place of our younger brother Emel who had died. My parents adopted Charlie, put him through school, and he is now a captain for Delta Airlines. *Sis*

Great Grandmother

My maternal Great Grandmother, an Eskimo named "Kwimiak" was born on Nelson Island, off the west coast of Alaska. In those days, the Russians were all along the coast, trading with the Eskimos and hunting seals and otter. My Great Grandmother had light eyes and hair but we were never able to determine how much Russian blood she had. Along the Bering Sea coast, you could tell many Eskimos had Russian heritage.

After my Great Grandmother moved to the village of Nunapitchuk, below Bethel on the Johnson River, Mom had her come to Akiak. Mom wanted her to stay with us but our diet wasn't what she was used to so she moved back to Nunapitchuk. Kwimiak was a great story teller and since we couldn't understand Eskimo, Mom would translate. Kwimiak would tell stories of long, long ago. She said that bowls, spoons, and cups were mostly made out of driftwood since there were no trees on Nelson Island.

I was quite small when she came to visit but can remember the Eskimo version she told of why bears have no tails. The story goes ... An Eskimo lady and her two sons were left in their snow igloo, while the husband went hunting. During the night they heard loud growling on the top of their igloo. There at the top where a smoke hole is, was a polar bear, trying to get in backwards. She and her sons were very frightened. They were burning seal-oil candles for cooking and light. They each grabbed one of the candles and burned the bear's bottom, along with its long tail. The bear ran off with a lot of noise from pain. She and her sons went out the next morning and there lay the dead polar bear with its tail completely burned

35

off. That is why the polar bear has no tail.

It is estimated by records that great-grandmother, Kwimiak, died around the age of 103. *Sis*

Birth and Early Memories

I was born April 8, 1927 at the government hospital, on the other side of the river. I was born the third oldest, after my sister Hanna and brother Arthur or "Sonny" as we called him. I don't have many memories of my early childhood. A few incidences have lingered in my mind, however.

In the early years, tuberculosis was rampant in most Alaska villages and took many lives. My mother's sister Bessie contracted the disease as she attended the government school on the other side of the river. Aunt Bessie died at an early age and I remember how all the villagers came to her funeral. I re-

Butch holds his lead dog Jimmy. We used to go on Sunday drives with our dog team. Butch trained an incredible, intelligent, lead dog named Trouble.

member my father guiding the horse, with the coffin on a sled, back to the cemetery. It remains in my mind that the folks said Ruby, her daughter, was 3 years old at the time and I was the same age. Our folks took over and she moved in with us. We had inherited a new sister and she was raised right along with us.

Papa and Uncle Reno had a fox and mink farm in the early years. I remember following Papa around while he fed the animals. One day I misused an axe and cut my hand badly. Papa was rushing me home and passed the school house. The teacher, hearing my wails, had him bring me into the school where classes were in session. She and Papa bandaged and fixed me up. It healed well but I still bear the scar.

Joe Venes, Gyda, and Pauline on a trip to the reindeer camp with Joe's team of dogs.

My mother made me a beautiful mink parka with a wolf ruff. There were tassels at intervals decorated with wolverine. On each red and white yarn tassel, hung a dime. Mom had Papa drill a hole in each dime. I can remember chewing on those dimes and Mom said I teethed on them.

While we were small and growing up, we always had some girl helping Mom around the house with the chores. There were diapers to be washed and house cleaning to be done. After Mom lost her sister Bessie to tuberculosis, she was always extra careful and afraid of all contagious diseases.

When we had visitors from contaminated houses, the dishes were boiled or washed with Clorox water after they were used. There always seemed to be a pot of boiling water on the stove. We had one certain maid, about 16 or 17 years old, from a village. She was a happy girl and liked to tease. I got so attached to her, more so than to my mother because Mom was always busy. I don't remember her English name but her Eskimo name was "Aunghoos." She stayed right in our home with us. She'd dance the Eskimo dance and tried to teach me how. I did quite well and enjoyed dancing.

The older boys at Akiak liked to tease her, too. One day Willie Chaney, Raymond Anderson, and Andrew Miller, came running into our house, dragging this little Laplander with a bald head. One boy grabbed her and the others sat Ole Polk on her lap and made them kiss. Of course I was crying. I thought they were hurting her. I was holding onto her skirt and Mom, hearing all the commotion, came to rescue "Aunghoos'" and chased them all off. My happiness was short lived, however. Not long after, her folks sent for their daughter to come home and in a few days a boat came for "Aunghoos." In the early days, planned marriages were made by Eskimo families, and that was why she had to go home. The

Gyda and Joe Venes Jr. out on the trail looking at reindeer.

world seemed to come to an end for me. I was so unhappy and seems I just couldn't part from her. The potatoes had just been planted by the river bank. When they took her I pitched a fit, crying and rolling in the potato patch. No one could console me. I never saw her again. After she married, she died at an early age. Anyway, a good batch of potatoes came up that year.

I remember Papa hitching up the dog sled and bundling Mama and us kids up in warm clothes and taking us to the other side of the river. Joe Williams had a store and pool hall where silent movies were shown, mostly Charlie Chaplin and cowboy pictures. There was also a piano in Joe's store. Sarah Percy would play it during intermissions. She worked hard at the peddles and it amazed us all.

We had 12 good husky dogs and a large basket sled we used to travel from one village to the next, or on Sunday drives. Papa trained our lead dog, Jimmy, very well. Whenever we met another team coming on the same trail, Jimmy would lead our team off the trail so the other dog team could pass without any trouble. If we happened to lose the sled, Jimmy would turn the team around at our command. He lived to an old age and prior to his death, Butch trained another lead dog named "Trouble." "Trouble" was just like Jimmy, another incredible, intelligent, lead dog.

Sis

Carl I. Carlsen's warehouse and summer mail plane.

Bessie, Catherine, and Dorothy swim in the Kuskokwim River near Carlsen's boat.

Trading Post

C arl I. Carlson, a Norwegian from Norway, ran a trading post and the village post office on our side of the river. Lovely log living quarters were attached to the back of the store and post office. He had a couple of storage caches, and a hand-railed car to transport supplies from the river bank to the store and large warehouses. Carl ordered his groceries and supplies from Seattle.

Carl I. Carlsen's Trading Post and warehouse.

They arrived in Bethel in the spring on the steamship "Tupper." The sternwheeler, "Tana" brought the freight to Akiak from Bethel. He also bought and sold raw furs of all kinds, and the dried salmon people fed to their sled dogs.

Coastal boats brought seal pouches or "pokes" as we called them filled with seal oil. Carl dug a hole close to his warehouse and filled it with cold

41

water, to keep the stored seal oil pouches as fresh as possible. It was a popular item for the Native people who liked seal oil. The cold water served as a refrigerator.

I barely remember Mrs. Carlson, his wife. She died when I was very young but I remember her being so sick. Before she passed away, Carl sent for his niece, Gyda Eide, from Norway to help with the house and store. Gyda was around 16 and couldn't speak English but she caught on quickly with us helping her and before long, she was like one of us and joined us

in games, dog team rides, swimming and ice skating. Eventually Gyda had her own five-dog team.

Mrs. Ole Anderson and Gyda started a sewing club. Each week we'd gather at different homes for a night of sewing, embroidering, knitting and crocheting. To complete the evening we'd have a

Carl I. Carlsen's Trading Post in 1934 with fox and mink pelts.

treat with our coffee. Sometimes we'd have a guest who was passing through to tell his experiences. One night our visiting guest was Jay Cooke, who come up with his dog team from Bethel. Jay was always dressed in beautiful parkies and mukluks. For the evening treat, we had hand churned ice cream and chocolate waffles made over a wood stove. The waffle iron was made to exactly fit over a removed round stove lid. We had to watch the waffles carefully so they didn't burn. We turned the waffle iron over and over until the waffle was done. Jay Cooke was thrilled with such a treat, but was quite nervous and frustrated around so many women. While he was cutting his waffle, it went off the plate and onto his lap, such an embarrassment for poor Jay. All of us younger girls giggled and giggled. I'm sure that's why he never accepted an invitation like that again. *Sis*

Old Timers

The men who came into the country, all came about the same time, mainly settling along the Kuskokwim River. Most of them had large families like ours and became close friends. We visited often, mostly during the summer months as boating was much easier than traveling by dog team in the winter.

These men were miners, traders, mail carriers, or reindeer herders. Some settled as far up the river as McGrath, the headwaters of the Kuskokwim. They hauled their own freight with boats or barges, and met the steamship, from Seattle, at the Bethel port.

Joe Jean settled at Goodnews Bay and Oscar Samuelson at Oscarville,

Old-timers, Fred Chaney, Johnny Hitz, Neil Corrigal, Clyde Hunter, and Willie Chaney in the back. Sig Hopstad, Papa, and Mama in front.

below Bethel. Those who lived in Bethel were Oscar Hall, Chris Nerby, Charles Jacobsson, Alex Hately, Jack Smeaton, Big Hans, Neil Corrigal,

Ole Hofseth, Ed Stevenson, Louis Moncher, Dad Brown, Tom Conquest, Mr. Link, Tony Sumi, and Ed McCann. Harry Samuelson lived in Akiachak, east of Akiak. In Aniak or surrounding areas, lived Harry Alain, George Morgan, Harry and Jack Brink, George Hoffman, George Fredericks, Dennis Parent, Nick Mellick, and Chris Dahl.

There were a few large families at McGrath. They included the Koenigs, Vanderpools, Gurtlers and Dave Andersons, Jack McGuire, a bar owner and poker player-bachelor who always smoked big cigars. Ed Miller had a barging company out of McGrath and was called the "Hootananee Kid."

On our side of the river at Akiak, lived Joe DeMantle, Joe Chaney, Sig Hopstad, Joe Venes, Ole, and Alfred Anderson, Jens Kvamme, Wilfred Reno, Little Hans, the Sara brothers: Peter, Michael, and Clement and our Dad. These were the actual men who married, settled and raised families in these particular areas. *Sis*

Mr. Reeth

There was an old gentleman name Reeth. I think his first name was Warner. He had no known relatives and was from Finland. We called him the "Colonel." He always walked so straight with a hat and cane. Reeth had about 160 acres behind the village that was covered with beautiful raspberries and currents. We were always a little afraid of him and would sneak onto his property to go skating on his lakes—always three or four of us together. Sometimes we'd get brave and go with our father when he went back to see Reeth about something. Reeth had a small house halfway in the ground, with the windows bordering the ground. He had a bed that was built in the wall and handmade tables and stools. Reeth had extra wooden gas-can boxes to sit on and to use for his cupboards, too. It was an interesting house to go into and to see insulation made of old foreign newspapers and cardboard boxes. Reeth called his property "The Vossaborg" and had a posted sign to that effect.

One summer Reeth sent for a mail-order bride from "Outside," as we called the Lower 48 states. With his boat and oars, he rowed all the way to Bethel from Akiak to claim her as his bride. She was to arrive on the steamship "Tupper" from Seattle. The story is that she took one look at him, saw him for what he was, and turned right around and went back to Seattle on the same ship. I heard that in communicating with him, he told a lot of stories that she believed. Reeth had gone so far as to build a new house for her. It wasn't much to look at but it was a house. He never lived in it and called it his summer home. Apparently it was built with no insulation.

Our Side of the River

During the summer, someone was always hiding on Reeth's property picking his berries. Since us kids travelled together, we always posted a guard to spot him so we could all run and hide. Reeth had a large drainage ditch grown over with willows. We'd always jump into it and hide. He'd come right over our heads on the bridge, so we wouldn't breathe or make a move. Reeth caught a few berry poachers. Karen, the little Lapp lady, was one but she didn't speak English. He'd yell at her for picking his berries and grab her buckets and spill them on the ground. She'd be frightened and run home. Sometimes he'd catch us, too, but we'd make it home since we ran faster than he did. When we got older we'd answer him back. One day Ruby, Elias, Butch, and I got caught but we put up a good front. He was calling everyone names and when I chimed in, he called me a "Bulldozer." We always had a lot of jam and jelly so didn't need his berries anyway. Reeth had good looking vegetable gardens. We never raided his patch, as we knew he used his own body waste as fertilizer. Sis

Dentists

It was bad luck for anyone who suffered from a toothache. There were traveling dentists who would only come once in a while during the year. If we had a toothache, we'd use home remedies to kill the pain-cloves and a strong herb and even a bit of tobacco stuffed into the cavity. Sometimes someone would have to go to the other side of the river to see Dr. Myers, and that meant having a tooth extracted. No one liked to go to him unless they really had to.

One day Uncle Reno came to town with his barging scow. His deckhand Willie Moonface had a swollen jaw from a toothache. Reno took Willy to see Dr. Myers and while he removed the tooth, we could hear Willy yelling halfway across the river. I guess Dr. Myers didn't deaden it enough. Willy complained the doctor almost pulled his whole jaw out. Of course, we kids were so scared after, we really used our toothbrushes regularly.

Dr. Broflat was one of the visiting dentists. He didn't seem much better than Dr. Myers. Dr. Bart LaRue was another dentist. Everyone thought we were related as we pronounced our name the same, but we weren't. Dr. LaRue had his own airplane so we called him the "Flying Dentist." He flew out of Fairbanks, down the Yukon River, and up the Kuskokwim stopping at each village to work on teeth. Other dentists would come but Drs. Broflat and LaRue were the most frequent and dependable. *Sis*

Pioneer Meetings

Carl I. Carlson held a pioneer meeting for the area every winter at his home. The old timers from up and down the river would arrive. Jack McQuire from McGrath was a professional poker player, Nick Mellick from Sleetmute, George Hoffman from Napaimute, Jack and Harry Brink from Flat/Aniak, Jack McDonald, Harry Allain of Kalskag, and Harry Samuelson from Akiachak. From Bethel came Neil Corrigal, Oscar Hall, Chris Nerby, Lewis "Shorty" Moncher, "Pinkie" Seakanoff, Ed McCann, and Chris Dahl. Also

Bethel's first dog team race to Akiak and return, 1937. As I remember, Max Lieb was the winner and Johnny (Cocoa) York was second.

other miners from Nyac—including the older men from Akiak. A good time was had which included card playing, shooting pool and discussing politics. During the 1930s, James Wickersham was the territorial governor, followed by Anthony Diamond and Ernest Gruening.

A nice dinner was prepared by Gyda, Carl's niece. After the meeting and dinner, the music began. The Frenchmen sang their songs in their native tongue, followed by Irish songs accompanied by Scotty Morrison on the fiddle. It was a jovial time. *Sis*

Laplanders

The Laplanders had a large herd of reindeer, at the foothills of the Alaska Range behind Akiak, . The Sara's settled at Akiak, among other Laplander families including Lars Nelson, Ole Poke, Per Spein and Pete Seri. The men would constantly come from the foothills to check on their families. They'd travel with small fast sleds pulled by reindeer. The herders were always dressed so colorful in reindeer skin parkies, hats, and lapboots bordered with red yarn decorations and turned up toes. Their colorful clothing fascinated us. We kids liked to have them come as they gave us fast, exciting rides with their sleds and reindeer. They were very good skiers, too.

The government, or BIA, brought out reindeer herds from the Laplanders in about 1937. The herds were all scattered around Alaska—at Akiak, Naknek, Unalakleet and Nome.

Our father and other men of the village would go back to the hills for our meat supply. Papa would hitch the dogs to a large basket sled and come back loaded down with reindeer meat. Reindeer was ten dollars a carcass then. Papa would hang our supply in the woodshed and it looked like a

51

slaughter house. During winter the meat stayed frozen until it was used.
. When the weather started warming up in early spring, we'd be busy
canning and drying meat for summer use. It was a treat when Papa would
hand grind meat for hamburger and meat loaf. It was very tasty.

In the early 1930s there were no moose in the lower river areas. We'd
have to go way up river to hunt them. During the summer and early fall,
all the men were at their jobs so there was no one to go hunting. Sometimes
a friend would stop, coming down river, who had been lucky on their hunt

and present us with
a nice piece of
moose. It was a great
treat to have a nice
moose roast or steak,
since our main meat
diet was reindeer.

Peter and Christina
Sara always had
racks of dried rein-
deer meat. In the
early spring, they'd
start drying meat for
storage. We kids
were forever raiding
their meat racks.
They knew we were
doing it, but we were
never caught in the
act. We kids liked to

**The Laplanders, Alfred Anderson, Naknek
Herder, Lars Nelson, Ed McCann, and Mike
Sara, in the back row, left to right. In the front
row, left to right, is Per Spein, Ole Polk, Per
Ante, Peter Sara, and his wife, Christine.**

visit them as we knew they would treat us with dried meat. Sometimes
Christina would give us a piece of candy. Christina was a great question-
asker. We'd make a game of who totaled the most questions. A typical
question was "What is your Mama doing?"

Peter and Christina Sara had one child named Mary, a girl our Aunt
Bessie's age. She and Aunt Bessie went to school on the other side of the
river, before the Territorial school opened. They both contracted Tuberculosis, Consumption, as it was called then, and died about the same time
in 1931.

Two little Laplanders, brother and sister to Christina, lived in a house
close to Peter Sara's. They stood about 4 feet 8 inches tall. His name was
Ante and hers was Karen. Karen loved to come visit Mom. She'd appear
when we least expected, without knocking, and place herself on a chair in
our house. Mama was always unhappy when she came. Karen had a bad
habit of spitting on the floor and wiping it with her Lapp boots. Since Mom

had lost her sister Bessie to tuberculosis, she was always worried about germs. Each time Karen would visit she'd do the same thing even if Mom tried to explain that she shouldn't. Mom would treat her to tea, bread or "asalyak" (fried bread). When Karen left, she'd repeat her bad habit and then leave for home. Mom would get out the clorox and scrub brush. The habit of sanitizing after visitors, applied to the Eskimo people who came from the other side where Tuberculosis was so prevalent, too. Mom would constantly be boiling dishes and cups they had used. We seemed to always use a lot of clorox. With the TB scare, we kids were never allowed to visit homes that may have the disease. Despite epidemics that came and went, we all turned out to be healthy.

Laplander, Per Spein

Ole Poke was a short Laplander and he had a bald head. We kids of the village would constantly tease him, but he seemed to always enjoy it. Ole would make trips to the river bank to carry water with a neck yoke and a couple of buckets. Sometimes it would take him all day to make one trip. One of the kids would see him coming and inform the others. While someone teased him and he'd give chase, another would spill his buckets. It seemed a ritual as a few days later he'd come down for more water and the same trick was repeated. In the winter, we'd have snowball fights. The older kids would grab Ole and rub snow on his bald head. He was a fast runner and sometimes would catch one of the kids then he'd get even. This teasing was great entertainment for us. We all knew he enjoyed it, too. If he didn't see any kids for a few days, he'd come looking for us.

Besides Peter Sara, his brothers, Michael and Clement, lived there with families of their own. Clement and Martha had three children: Marita, Martin and a baby boy who died with either whooping cough or diphtheria. They moved to Bethel when their kids got older and Clement and Martha then had more children. Michael Sara had a home at Akiak. His wife died. He then sent his two daughters, Helen and Julia to the Moravian Mission Children's Home at Kwethluk, a village below Akiak. When they got old enough to come home, he enrolled them in school with us. Mike was a great entertainer with his old stories

The herders were always dressed so colorful in reindeer skin parkies, hats, and lapboots bordered with red yarn decorations and turned up toes.

of past experiences. I remember him telling us about his skiing days. Having no transportation, he took out his skis and skied to Bethel in "one hour and sixty minutes." Of course, that always brought on a good laugh. The government, or BIA, bought reindeer herds from the Laplanders around 1937. The herds were all scattered around Alaska—at Akiak, Naknek, Unalakleet and Nome. Karen and Per Ante passed away before then, also a younger Sara brother named Mortan died at an early age, in Akiak. Michael and Peter Sara remained in Akiak but Clement moved with his family to Bethel. Ole Poke, Lars Nelson and Peter Sara moved to Naknek, and Per Spein passed away. As the years passed, the others left us. *Sis*

Toys

Not many toys were bought from stores. What we had was usually handmade by our father or mother. Papa made small sleds for sledding or to hitch a dog or two, in order to pull us around. We all enjoyed the sleds but our favorite for sliding was an old piece of cardboard, an old shovel or even an old discarded pan. They seemed to go down the hill faster. We had one sturdy wagon and one good sled we all used. Papa made double runner skates for us beginners. They tied right to our shoepacs which was our main source of winter footwear, besides mukluks. Sonny was the first to own a pair of skates, made in the Holland style with turned up toes. He was able to skate faster than anyone else which made us all envious. It reminded us of "Hans Brinker and His Silver Skates." The boys also had a red scooter which we all shared in the summertime.

We girls spent a lot of time making miniature rag dolls. We'd make complete families and play with them, just as the kids do nowadays with Barbie dolls. The Eskimo name for them is "Inugoeks." We played many hours with them. Hanna was given the first store-bought doll with a plaster head. Hanna and her friend, Catherine, were older than us younger girls and they liked to run away and play by themselves. Well, one day we had a fight and I grabbed her doll and broke its head. We were never spanked but the folks gave me a great scolding. I was so ashamed and seemed punished enough, spending a lot of time trying to make it up to Hanna for breaking her doll. Eventually she forgave me, I think.

At Christmas we always got two gifts each which were nicely wrapped. There was something nice to wear that we needed and then a special toy. The boys got model airplanes or boats to build and a game of some kind. We girls got jewelry, homemade dolls or something knitted. Mom made a lot of knitted socks, sweaters, caps, neck scarves and mittens for Christmas. They were well made.

Our Papa built two sturdy swings out in the yard, in two different sizes. It gave us a lot of pleasure over the years, swinging to our hearts content.

We also built homemade stilts to walk on around our neighborhood. They were quite a novelty until we got tired of playing with them. We were never lacking for toys and play items. *Sis*

Electricity, Boats, and Supplies

There was no electricity—gas lamps, kerosene lamps and lanterns were used. About 1941 Papa got a generator. We did a lot of canning, salting salmon bellies in brine barrels, drying and curing fish, and preserving, in cans, fresh meat and fresh salmon. We also used mason jars as well, there was so much food to preserve.

There were two steamships from Seattle during the summer months. One arrived in the spring and one in the fall. They moored at Bethel where sternwheelers and barges met the ships unloading freight, groceries or whatever people had ordered from "outside." The sternwheelers, fully loaded, made deliveries at all the villages along the Kuskokwim river. My folks always had a big order of groceries—cases of canned vegetables, flour, sugar, cereal, dried fruit, coffee, tea, Spam, Crisco, rice, canned fruit, and dried milk. We mixed the dried milk with water and it was called Klim. Eggs came in wooden cases that were stored in our root cellar for winter use. We had to worry and care for them. Papa kept turning the cases around so the yolks wouldn't stick to the shells, and they had to be candled when used. Then we had to break them one at a time before using to make sure they weren't spoiled. When we ran out of them, we used dried or powdered eggs.

We always had butter on hand. It was packed in a keg full of brine. Even after World War II, when everyone else seemed to be using margarine, we had real butter. We didn't like margarine as we had to mix coloring into it to make it look like butter, and it wasn't nearly as tasty. We always had sourdough hot cakes for breakfast. They don't taste as good unless you have real butter and homemade syrup.

We all welcomed the sternwheelers- "The Tana," "Wallace Langley" and the "Northwestern." We could see the smoke before the actual boats came around the bend of the river. The older boys of the village usually worked on the sternwheelers. We got to know the crew. Captain Roy Atkins and engineer Ikie Hayes were the ones I remember.

The sternwheeler, Wallace Langley hauling freight and passengers up the Kuskokwim River.

All the kids gathered on the banks where they threw apples and oranges to us. Later when the crew was through unloading, we'd be invited on board to roam around and be treated royally in the kitchen. *Sis*

School

Akiak Territorial School was built and maintained by Grandpa Venes. The one-room school included living quarters for the teachers. There were separate two-holed outhouses out back for the boys and girls, and a woodshed loaded with wood for the basement and kitchen stoves. When school first opened, I was still pretty young. I can remember the older kids being the Anderson boys. Aunt Nora, my sister Hanna, one or two of the Chaney boys and the children of Oscar Hall. He and his wife Anna had a trading post 5 miles below Akiak. They had a large family and sent those who were elementary age to Akiak, where they would board with the Anderson families for the school season. The school held about fifteen to twenty kids plus blackboards, desks, a large Alaska map, a small library and a picture of George Washington—a good spitball target.

Blanche Torgerson was my first grade teacher. She was a good teacher and I liked her very much. Our first duty, after the bell rang, was to raise the flag on the flagpole. Someone was assigned for a couple of weeks at a time for flag duty. Then came the pledge of allegiance to the flag and we would sing the Alaska song or the Star Spangled Banner. Once a month we'd be herded to the trading post to get weighed as we had no scale at the school. We would measure the heights of everyone, too. Miss Torgerson stayed for a couple of years and left for Valdez where she met a man named Sullivan and got married.

Beth Anderson was our next teacher. Her father was a U. S. Marshal at Bethel. Beth taught about 2 years at Akiak but we didn't get much of an education from her. She was young, used a lot of makeup, dressed fancy and used high-heeled shoes. She was popular with the eligible bachelors and pilots. Leo Moore was flying then. He visited Akiak and their love blossomed. When he'd fly over the school she'd drop everything, even in the middle of a lesson, and down to the river bank she'd run. One spring day she forgot to put on decent shoes and while running down to the river bank she got her feet stuck in the mud and one heel broke. We had our heads stuck out of the school windows, laughing. She was so mad at all of us. My father was the shoe repairman so he had more work to do. Don't

Teacher Agnus Schlosser and her students, Bessie, Blassa Paul, Rolf Gardner, Cutie, Martin Sara, Glenn Gardner in the front row. Jack Kawagley, Marita Sara, Robert Gardner, Sis, Ruby, Catherine, and Butch in the back row.

you know, George Washington really got the spitballs that time. Leo Moore always brought a bag of candy for all of us at school. At those times, Aunt Nora was put in charge until school was let out for the day. Leo and Beth were married after her school year was completed.

William Parks taught after Beth. He was a heavy-set bachelor and was a good teacher. After Beth Anderson taught us, he had to set most of the students back a year. We kids would visit him in the evenings just to listen to him tell ghost stories. Some were very gruesome. At the end of the evening we'd all be afraid to go home, and so we'd leave and stick together. The Kawagley kids, who lived at the last house in the village, would be afraid to walk alone. Papa would feel sorry for them at times and walk them home. On the trail enroute to Kawagley's was the home of a little

Lapp lady, who had previously died. Before the kids even got to her empty house, they'd take off running, not looking to the left or right.

Bill Parks left at the end of that school year and retired on Kodiak Island. Gladys Wilbur was next. She taught for a year and then transferred to Unalakleet where she met a man named Trager and married him.

The year the Akiak Territorial School opened, Agnes Schlosser was the first teacher. Later she decided to came back to Akiak and she taught us for another 4 years.

Elias, Ruby, Bessie, Alice, Agnus, Sis, Catherine, Martin Sara, Cutie, Betty Clark, Merita Sara, Butch, Olof Hopstad, and Jackie Kawagley.

Mr. and Mrs. John Naas came next, during World War II. Peggy Naas taught at Haycock previously, where she met John and then came to Akiak. They were a nice couple and she was a good teacher. The Red Cross sent a bunch of yarn to the school for the purpose of making socks, sweaters, scarves, mittens and caps, for the soldiers abroad. We older girls all knit, aside from our lessons. Peggy Naas had only one arm. She had lost it in an accident as a young girl. It didn't seen to bother or hinder her, though. She'd teach and listen to the lessons, while holding one needle under one arm and knitting with the other, not even missing a stitch. She was an admirable person.

Eleanor Smith, from Dillingham, was the last teacher at Akiak. Most of us graduated by 1943 and were gone. After that, the school was closed—there was not enough students to keep the school open.

I recall during our school years we'd have to have school pictures

The Class of 1932: Nora, Raymond Anderson, Patrick Smith, Gene Snow, Melvin Anderson, Ilene Snow, Front Row: Sonny, Ruby, Hanna, Sis, Rolf, Elias, and Wilfred

taken periodically. Scotty Auld, a miner who worked at the Nyac Mine and a Scotsman, was the photographer. He always seemed to be traveling from Akiak to Bethel taking family group pictures. We kids disliked having him come as he took forever preparing for the picture. He had a camera complete with a curtain on a pedestal, from which he ran to and fro. He was a perfectionist; somebody's head wasn't turned right, a collar had to be fixed, a shirt needed buttoning or the light wasn't quite right. When the picture was finally completed we were all worn out from so much posing and what not. The picture always turned out well and we couldn't complain because he was the only photographer we had.

There were no high schools unless we went to board at Bethel. Hanna, Ruby, Butch, and I all started working as soon as we were able. The younger ones—Bess, Lena, and Charlie, were the lucky ones to go on to higher grades. *Sis*

Chores

fter we girls became older, there were no extra helpers. As soon as we were old enough to peel potatoes we had to help with the cooking and the necessary housework. When dinner was over we had to clear the table, wash and dry dishes and sweep the floors. One week, one person was elected to a certain duty and we'd trade off. Of course, there were the bedrooms to take care of along with mopping the floors. Saturday was the complete cleanup day. No mops were used. We had to get down on our knees, get the scrub brush out, and wash in the corners and under the furniture. Arguments would get out of hand as it seemed no person wanted to do any more than the next. We went to drawing straws from the broom. That worked out okay until someone drew the same straw too many times. We got careless with the dishes and broke so many that Mom figured she'd teach us a lesson. She announced that if anyone broke a glass or plate again, we'd have to pay for it. Ten cents was the charge. In those days, ten cents was like a quarter today. Ruby paid heavily one evening. While setting the dining room table she stubbed her toe. She and all the dishes flew. About seven dishes were broken so Mom collected on that bunch.

Bess, and Lena, "Cutie," were much younger and Mom didn't insist they do too much. When Bess got a little older, we wanted her to help with the dishes. Anyway, Bess wasn't too happy about that. She rebelled until one of us would grab her and drag her to the dish pan while another rubbed her hands in the soapy water. She'd finally give up and do them. She also detested emptying the chamber pots. Now she's a better housekeeper than all of us. One day while I was rushing through the double doors to empty the chamber pot, I ran into Melvin Anderson. After that, he nicknamed me "Pee-Pot Sue."

Water had to be heated for washing clothes and diapers. We used rain or river water. We'd wash the smaller items and diapers over the washboard and hang them out on the lines to dry. In the winter, we'd hang them in the house. The kitchen area had a place for that, also one large bedroom had lines to dry clothes. A good-sized storage room located upstairs had clothes lines for extra and bulky items. We had a large round wooden washing machine with a hand wringer attached, and a stick handle on top to push the agitator back and forth. That took a lot of muscle, and one person on each side to properly wash large bulky items such as heavy blankets, sheets, towels, and men's work clothes. Then all clothes were rinsed twice in two galvanized tubs. Our girlfriends, who didn't have as many chores, would come over and give us a hand. Catherine, Alice, Augusta and Helen would help just so we could hurry up and go outside to play.

There was a day set aside for mending and one for ironing too. I despised ironing and still do, but couldn't get away from it. The sad irons were heated on the kitchen stove. To get done in a hurry, we'd each iron an item and it didn't seem too much of a chore that way, taking turns.

Mom would get mad at me for tearing my panties. We wore dresses a lot in the summer but playing rough with marbles and making tree houses, I was forever getting them caught somehow. Mom complained because there was far too much sewing being done so Papa decided he'd do something about it. He went over to the store and bought me a couple of size 40 bloomers to wear. They seemed so noticeable because the elastic on the legs hung down close to my knee. I was made to wear them. They were embarrassing to wear, but needless to say I did learn to be more careful.

At an early age, my brothers learned to work with Papa cutting wood and taking care of the animals. Sonny was the oldest. He and his friend, Rolf Anderson, decided to cut wood to sale for ten dollars a cord. They sold it to anyone who would pay the price but it was mostly to the storekeeper. When Butch and Elias got older, they were doing the same. We were all trying to find a way to earn money. Sometimes we helped Papa at his sawmill, cutting fire wood or building logs for sale.

The Chaney boys, with their dad, would go beaver trapping during the winter. Jimmy Downey would go, too, and so would a large man named Jack O'Keefe. Sonny went with them a few times and I can remember them coming home with stacks of beaver blankets. They were sold to the trading post or to the traveling fur buyers "Johnny Muskrat," Sam Applebaum or Norman Goldberg.

The teacher, or store owner, would hire us girls to come and clean their houses for about a dollar for a day's work. At the store were shoes and cotton dresses for one dollar each. We'd always find something we wanted at the store and spend our wages.

One day at the store, Ruby and I, seeing no one around, loaded our pockets with candy, from a display case out of an open container. All of a sudden the storekeeper appeared. He said sternly "put that back." We were punished by having to work for what we did. The folks always knew what we were up to. No doubt Carl I. told them about it. It was never made an issue, though. They figured we'd learn through experience, which we did. *Sis*

A Day At The Woodcamp

My father, and his helper Middy, set up a woodcamp about 3 miles below Akiak where they'd spend the weekends cutting trees for building or firewood. They hauled the logs with Barney, the horse, or used a team of dogs. My brothers, Sonny and Butch, would be up early and ready to go. The sourdough hot cakes were made and a lunch was packed for the day. Sometimes one of us girls would be asked to go along. It was good to get away from the house for the day. There, in camp, was a tent set up with a small stove to warm up by or to fire-up for making coffee or tea for lunch. It was just like a picnic.

Papa and Middy coming from the woodcamp.

There wasn't much we could do at the woodcamp, so, we'd go looking for spruce gum. The spruce trees have a pitchie sap that comes from under the bark. We discovered that if we collected the sap and chewed it, it would soften up like gum. It even had a sweet taste. We'd chip off a lot of spruce gum and take it home to enjoy later. This saved us from having to buy gum at the store.

Papa plowing gardens with Barney the horse. Bessie and Dorothy help hold down the plow.

We also looked for birch trees with a growth called "punk." We cut the punk off and filled gunny sacks. Oscar Samuelson, the trader from Oscarville, paid us five dollars a sack. It was a good way to make money. He sold it at his store to the Eskimos. We had quite a business going. The Eskimos burned the punk and mixed the ashes with their chewing tobacco to make it stronger. Later we heard it

Laplander Ole Polk, Sis, Joe Chaney Sr., Ruby, Wilfred Reno, David Twitchell, Johnny Hitz, Papa, Joe Venes Jr. Ed McCann is in the sled taking off for Bethel.

gave them a little high similar to a drug when it was mixed as such.

I was quite a tomboy and close to my brothers. I preferred being outside with them piling wood in the woodshed, throwing wood down the basement shoot for the furnace or just sitting on a log to keep it steady while they hand-sawed the wood. I would keep them laughing by telling funny stories or jokes so the work didn't seem to be such drudgery. *Sis*

Eskimo People and Dances

O n the other side of the river were some Eskimo families. John Egoak had a big family. He was also the Chief. He had great power among the people. He'd arrange marriages for his sons and daughters. The families I remember, besides his, were; the Jacksons, Williams, Lakes, Owens, Waskas. Ivans, Cornelius, and the Kawagleys.

In the early 1930s the Eskimos held meetings and Eskimo dances. They were held in a round, underground hut made of mud and logs called a "qasigik". When the main dances were held, people from the surrounding villages would come. There was always a big feast afterwards. My family would attend. We loved to go to watch the dancing and singing. The men did the singing and drumming on large seal-gut drums which they beat in time with the singing.

Women did the dancing. The dances told stories about their way of life, and with hand gestures, their stories were dramatized. The dancers held dance fans accented with feathers or fringes of reindeer hide. Sometimes a man would join the women and he would dance on his knees. The best dancers were, Mrs. Eddie Owens, Mrs. Roland, " Rosie" Women, Molly Owens, and Mrs. Lake. Other women took turns, too.

The missionaries put a stop to the dances. They said our dances were sinful and heathenistic. The Eskimo language was also forbidden in the BIA schools. Over the last ten years or so, the language and culture has been encouraged. Hopefully the people won't forget their traditional values again.

John Snow and his wife were teachers at the government school. They had a son, Gene, and a daughter, Ilene. They were always visiting on our side of the river —joining us for games and other activities. The Snow family was there for quite a while until Mr. Snow got a position in Bethel, in charge of the BIA. It was at this time that the Laplanders sold their herds of reindeer to the BIA, too. John Snow was the reindeer superintendent for the BIA when the transaction between the Laplanders and the government was made. The year was 1937. *Sis*

Games

Usually, in the late afternoon or evenings of spring and summer, was the time to play games. We played marbles, jump rope, or "Anti-I-Over." Anti-I-Over was a game with two opposing teams of players. We'd pick a roof of someone's shed or home which was just the right height to throw a ball over. When it was caught on the other side, the catcher would run around to the other side and tag one of the players with the ball. If a player was tagged, they were out. When there were no players left on one side, the other team was the winner.

A game called "Lap Game" was played. I think the Laplanders probably introduced it into this country; therefore, the name. Two teams were formed, each picked partners plus a pitcher. It was a form of baseball but we used softballs instead. If you caught the ball that was pitched, your team would get an extra score. If their catcher caught the ball and hit the runner with it, that runner was out. There were two goals. We played that game a lot. I always liked to be on the boys side, since I was always a tomboy.

With the help of us kids, the storekeeper cleared off a space in front of the store and set up a croquet and horseshoe set. When we got tired of playing one game, we'd switch to the other. There was a swimming hole in a slough up the beach. If the weather was nice, we'd go swimming everyday. The boys would build a big bonfire for warming-up and to keep the mosquitoes away, too. But even with all the swimming we did, I didn't turn out to be a very good swimmer.

During winter nights, we'd play games gathered around our round dining table. We played five-hundred, pig, monopoly, and sometimes we put puzzles together. The folks joined us in a lot of these games. Papa would get tickled when he'd beat mom at cards. He'd laugh and she'd get mad, the more he'd laugh the madder she got. It was really funny.

Mr. Carlson I. and Gyda would invite all of us over there to play Canasta or Chinese checkers. We'd go over quite often. At the end of the evening, we always knew it was time to go home when he'd start making shavings to start the morning fire. We liked to beat him at games, too. We knew he didn't like losing.

On cold moonlit nights, we'd dress warm, get a large basket-sled and go sliding down the river bank along with a load of kids. With a long hard push, we'd go downhill and were able to ride halfway across the river. We all worked hard pulling that sled back up—again and again. With so much fun no one complained of the hard work.

There were two girls from Tuluksak, which is 20 miles above Akiak. One was Emily Smith, whose father had a trading post. She was a half-sister to Patrick Smith of Akiak. She and her friend Della Bird liked to come to Akiak and spend a few days visiting. They were Aunt Nora's age. One evening when the girls from Tuluksak came down, they joined the lap-game. Emily was staying with Gyda. During the night Emily got very sick and she sent Gyda over to get Minnie Kawagley to help. Much to everyone's surprise, Minnie helped deliver a healthy baby girl for Emily. The delivery turned out fine despite nobody knowing about the pregnancy. *Sis*

Freighting and Pearl Harbor

Uncle Reno started freighting for the New York Alaska Gold Dredge Corporation (NYAC). With two boats and two 4 HP Johnson outboard motors, Reno started out from Bethel. Reno and his helpers went up the Tuluksak River, as far as they could go, to an upper landing. At the landing, a tractor met the boat and hauled the supplies to NYAC. His helpers were Willie Moonface, Andrew Miller, and Willie, son of Joe Chaney, from the mine. It took them about 2 weeks to complete one trip. Reno's freighting business continued all summer.

Reno's first barging outfit—2-4 HP Johnsons

A Japanese man by the name of Tony Sumi started a barging business, too. We all called him "Tony the Jap." He asked my father to work for him. We kids were pretty young then so Papa was happy to, then he could check on us at home. Akiak was on their route and they stopped at home all the time. My brother, Sonny, was old enough to start work so he and Middy

Chaney, Henry Nansen, and a few other deck hands from Bethel also went to work for Sumi.

The name of Sumi's boat was "The Mink." The boat had a cabin which

Seattle Steamship, The Tupper at Bethel.

included a kitchen and sleeping quarters for the crew, all in one room. The cook was Tony's sister-in-law named Mary. She became a good friend of ours and sometimes we girls would take turns going up the river with the boat, to help her cook. Hanna was hired as another cook one summer. We

Reno's boat. In the boat—Wilfred and Elias and swimming in the water Rolf, Adam, and Sonny.

liked to go on these trips. Tony and his wife, Sara, didn't have any children of their own but raised a few kids who needed homes. On one trip he brought a baby down from Tuluksak, a village above Akiak, and announced he bought the baby boy for a pound of Lipton tea. Tony had a kind heart so I'm sure other arraignments were made. We heard later the mother was a widow and couldn't afford to keep the baby. In the winter Sumi

74

would haul gravel by truck over the river ice, to build up the airport at Bethel, and sometimes do the same by barge in the summer. There was gravel located way up the Kuskokwim river.

When Pearl Harbor was bombed, December 7, 1941, Ben Kawagley, from the other side, came rushing over to tell the new but he got everything mixed up. He said the Japs had bombed Napaskiak, a village 5 miles below Bethel. Everyone got excited. Later we were alerted by radio that it was Pearl Harbor in Hawaii.

Tony Sumi, left, one of Tony's workers, center, and Papa, right.

It was so frightening. The village was alarmed and silent. The older villagers ordered everyone to keep things at a complete blackout at night. Dutch Harbor was bombed. The local boys were inducted into the service, one by one.

After Pearl Harbor, any Japanese who lived in Alaska was picked up and sent out to internment camps. Tony the Jap, had to leave his business and wife behind. Sara was an Eskimo woman with children. It was a sad

Tony Sumi's freighting barge the Mink. Hauling freight to Nyac.

farewell as the area residents thought the world of Tony. The older friends gave him a big farewell party at Bethel before he left. There was much sadness and tears. Tony never returned. He died in an Arizona camp and it was said that he died of a broken heart. *Sis*

Special Days

Every Fourth of July, practically the whole village would head up to the sandbar above Akiak for a celebration. Carl I. Carlson had a nice boat with a cabin that we liked to ride in. Papa had an inboard boat we called the "Took-Took" with a four-horsepower inboard motor. It held a lot of people. Others, who had boats, loaded them up with picnic supplies and we all spent the day playing—ball games, sack races, foot races, tug-of-war, and sack and leg wrestling. A big bonfire was made for cooking and to warm up by after swimming. It was so much fun and we didn't go home un-

Sis, Alice, Joe, Sonny, Catherine, Melvin, jumping the broom at the 4th doings, and Papa with his cigar.

til the last marshmallows were burned—a complete day of fun.

Halloween was another night we all enjoyed as we could pull pranks and get away with them. Everyone had out-houses with the wishbook, Sears Roebuck catalog, to be used for tissue. We turned over what outhouses we could. Good thing no one happened to be inside. Some, we piled high the inside with wood we did to some doorways. The older, braver boys went back to Mr. Reeth's and put a sled on his roof or stuffed his chimney with gunny sacks or grass. We hoisted up long-johns on the flagpoles and one time, someone got a hold of Beth Anderson's bloomers and strung them up—besides taping some to the blackboard. The boys

Mr. Carlsen, Ruby, Sis, Bessie, Dorothy, Martin Sara, Marietta Sara, Cutie, Jack Kawagley.

went into her quarters and placed live mice in a can by the door. When she arrived home with her escort after the dance—as the guilty ones reported—over went the can. She jumped up on a desk crying with fright and mascara running down her face.

Mrs. Christina Sara, Elizabeth Anderson, Minnie, Mrs. Smith, Nora, Dorothy Anderson, Mrs. Carlson, and Martha Sara. Front row— Ruby, Sis, Bessie, Hanna, Alice, Gyda, and Helen Sara.

One Halloween, Mike Sara's daughter, Helen, was staying with her uncle, Pete Sara and his wife, Christina, was out with us girls doing tricks. We raided the dried reindeer meat rack and found a pot with strong Lap boot grease in the outhouse. This grease was used to rub into boots to make them waterproof. We smeared that grease on the outhouse seats. After Helen had gone to bed, Pete had to go to the toilet. He went out and came back in swearing. He

Minnie and Gyda—Nora and Martha Sara— Hanna and Catherine—Elizabeth Anderson and Mrs. Ole Anderson.

had strong and vile smelling grease on his backside, and had to take a bath to get it off. Pete raised holy-heck with the boys for doing that. He never found out us girls were the culprits. The poor boys got all the blame. *Sis*

78

Airplanes

Around 1933, mail came to Akiak about once a month—by boat in the summer and dog team in the winter. Some carriers had twelve to fourteen strong dogs pulling a sled piled with mail. Different carriers took turns, but the ones I remember were Oscar Samuelson and his son, John, and Charles Jacobson. Oscar had the trading post 5 miles below Bethel. Beginning at Bethel, the teams would travel up the river leaving mail and packages at the villages along the Kuskokwim River as far as McGrath. When they reached McGrath, they would cross over to the Yukon River, delivering the mail as they came down the Yukon before crossing back over to Bethel.

Greeting Gillam's airplane with the mail—1940

I was 6 or 7 years old when the first airplane came to Akiak. School had just dismissed and my sister Ruby and I heard this loud noise overhead. All the huskies in the village started barking and howling. We got so frightened we hid under a porch. Looking up, we saw the first airplane—Harold Gillam from Fairbanks on his first mail run down the Kuskokwim. He landed on the river ice in front of the store. Gillam flew a one-motor Pilgrim. It made a very loud noise and carried a big load. He became our regular weekly mail carrier and he was very dependable, come rain or shine. We could set

Elias, Butch, Rolf, Olaf, Sis, Sonny, Bessie, and Dorothy.

our clocks by him!

More airplanes started carrying passengers, mail, or supplies. When anyone heard an airplane overhead they'd yell "airplane!" One of us kids would want to be the first to hear the drone so we could be the first to yell. We dropped what we were doing, except in school, and run down to the ice. We were right behind the postmaster, Carl I. Carlson, or a few

Pilot, Leo Moore, Beth Anderson, Matthew Egwok, Gyda, Mr. Mc Giverns, Carl I. Carlsen, Mrs. Mc Giverns, Mrs. Ole Anderson, Sis, Joe, Olaf Rolf, and Sonny. Front row—Bessie, Dorothy, Elias, and Butch. A farewell to school teacher, Elizabeth Anderson.

grown-up helpers, to greet the pilot. We got to know them all. We wanted to see what passengers were coming in and what was being delivered—anything for excitement.

During the summer months, airplanes landed on the sandy beaches. Each spring the men and older boys had to cut

down the willows and small trees, on the beach to prepare a small air strip.

Nat Brown's plane on sand strip.

That was the end of boat and dog team mail deliveries too. The old pilots were Johnny Littley, Leo Moore, Jack Peck, Nat Brown, Johnny Moore, Clarence Marsh, Merle Sasseen, Frank Barr Raymond Peterson,

Jack Jefford, Al Jones, and Harold Gillam. *Sis*

Gardens

Uncle Reno and my father owned two horses for heavy work: moving buildings, handling freight and wood, and plowing gardens. They were in big demand up and down the river. I don't remember the name of the horse that died just after they got him, but Barney lived to an old age. He was a good, gentle horse. We had fun riding him on the horse trail or around the village. After Barney died, they got another horse, it was a young horse named Dan. He was too feisty so they sold him to the Moravion Mission at Kwethluk.

Papa plowed all the village gardens and two large oat fields. I can remember those oat fields well because we played hide and seek in them—until we were run off.

There was a large basement under our house which was used as a root cellar for storing potatoes, other vegetables, and canned goods for the winter.

Weeding gardens was a real challenge. The mosquitoes were always bad and sometimes unbearable. Some summers the mosquitoes were worse than others. Headnets were used but were made of dark netting and were hard to see through. We girls wore long kuspuks, which are Eskimo summer parkies made of cotton material. They have a hood with a drawstring to pull close to your face to keep the bugs from your head and neck. Papa made smudge pots in which he burned green grass and were placed here and there while we weeded. The smudge pots were made from empty gas cans that were cut in half.

Keeping the gardens weeded was hard work, especially because we were in constant combat with those pesky mosquitoes. Our payoff came when the vegetables had grown large enough to eat. Us kids would sneak fresh vegetables from the gardens and we'd hide in some tall grass nearby, and eat to our hearts content. When we'd get caught, the fun was over—until the next time.

Gasoline came in five-gallon containers—two to a wooden case then. The empty cases, and gas cans, were always put to good use. You could go to almost anyone's house and pull up a wooden case to sit on, or see cupboards made of them. The cans were used to store nets, floats, or were cut in half for dog dishes.

Buhach, a substance burned in small portions, was used in homes to kill the mosquitoes or to keep them out. In homes, each bed would have a mosquito net properly sized, covering it to assure the sleeper a good night's sleep free of mosquitoes. When the war broke out in 1941, and soldiers were sent to Alaska, a troop sent to Bethel brought the first insect repellent. It was called "6-12" and was so strong it burned the skin when you put it on. But it kept the bugs away! *Sis*

Epidemics

As early as I can remember, tuberculosis was a threat to all of the village. Many Eskimos died and sometimes whole families were taken. It was because of the way they lived. The houses were small and the living quarters were tight—they had no fresh air flow. Our folks were very strict about any of us kids going on the other side of the river because of this. We were never allowed to eat in the homes there.

Around 1935 my brothers, Sonny and Butch, got scarlet fever. Dr. Meyers, the doctor at the BIA hospital on the other side of the river, came over and examined the boys. He was a small doctor with strong, thick glasses. He took out two large crisscross bone signs with "Quarantine" written in large letters and tacked them on the front and back doors of our house. We stayed home, without associating with any other families or attending school, for one month. The boys were isolated in one bedroom. They seemed to be sick for so long. Even after they recovered they took medicine to build up their blood and to regain their strength. It took them awhile to get over that illness and afterwards boils broke out on their neck several times. They were the only ones who got scarlet fever. Sonny and Butch wound up with heart murmurs but must have outgrown it because they passed their physicals when they went into the service.

Spinal meningitis came along in a few years and there were more deaths. Uncle Elias contracted the disease and Grandma Venes brought him to the new Bethel hospital. It was early fall, the doctor had a tent set up back on the tundra away from town, and treated Elias there. Grandma and nurse, Lulu Heron, stayed right with him until he finally got well. We credited Mrs. Heron with his survival. About 1940, red measles came along. People on both sides of the river came down with them. Our house was like a hospital with everyone sick except Papa and Joe Chaney. Between the two, they were kept busy taking care of us. One day a plane came over the house. We girls were curious to see who was coming. I opened the blinds to peek out, even when we were told to keep the blinds closed at all times. Apparently the brightness of the sun was too much and it weakened my eyes—I've worn glasses ever since. It so happened that Joe Chaney's oldest son, Willie, got married to Pauline Kameroff and they were coming to Akiak to make their home. Pauline quickly arrived at our house and assisted Papa with the children. She asked Willie to churn some ice cream. She hoped the coldness of the ice cream might reduce our fevers. We will never forget what a treat it was. I'm sure it put us on the mend.

Sometime during our years at school, we all got, what we called, the 7-year itch. The doctors sent a large supply of sulfur salve we smeared on ourselves daily. The folks were busy bathing us and constantly boiling our underwear. We got well and it didn't last for 7 years!

Lee Gardner moved his family to Akiak from the reindeer camp where he'd been working. They rented Little Han's house and stayed for a couple of years. Three of his boys attended school. Someone spotted lice in one of the boy's head at school, but it was too late. The whole school was infected. I think the remedy for getting rid of lice was to boil our underwear with a kerosene mixture and also to rub the kerosene mixture in our hair. Finally that was cleared up. After a few years, the Gardner family moved to Fairbanks.

During the red measles epidemic, our mother came down with diphtheria. She was kept isolated but our little brother, Emel, caught it and passed away. Our mother was stronger and able to fight off the infection. I remember them holding the funeral for Emel in our living room. Reverend Dittmer, from the Moravian church, officiated. He was the only minister available. Our brother, Sonny, who was working at Nyac, came down for the funeral and he came down with red measles, too.

A few years later our cousin, Wilfred, who was living with Grandpa Venes, caught diphtheria and passed away, before they were able to get him to the Bethel hospital.

Whenever there was a life-threatening disease in the households, we had to be quarantined. Those tragedies and moments in our life left an impact never to be forgotten. *Sis*

Christmas

We prepared for holidays well in advance. Well before Christmas arrived, Mom would bake the fruitcakes and we'd bake assorted batches of cookies. The Chaney boys always knew when we started baking cookies. They quit using our living room door to access our kitchen, but instead, used the door leading directly into the kitchen. These boys, with long arms, would cleverly pass by our cooling cookies and we'd wind up missing a lot of cookies. So we wised up and were always on the lookout for them.

The folks would start their home brew and then help us make root beer. We enjoyed making root beer as there wasn't much pop around then. Everything was bottled and ready for Christmas. We had plenty of candy, apples, and oranges. The folks ordered assorted nuts on the fall boat. They arrived in gunny sacks and we'd sit around our round table with small hammers breaking and eating nuts. The fresh fruits came by mail plane or by someone who was making a quick trip from Bethel by dog team.

Our Christmas tree was nicely decorated with ornaments, both home-made and store bought. Real candles in holders were clipped to the tree branches. Of course, we could never burn them unless the folks were there. The candles were always put out after we enjoyed them for a while—in fear of fire. Each year there was a school play. Everyone was invited. Santa gave out Christmas stockings—one year he almost got burned when his sleeve caught fire while bending too close to the candles on the tree. The fire was quickly put out. After the school play, we'd hold a dance, usually at our house since we had a large living room.

One night during the Christmas holidays, we had a dance at our house. A small decorated tree was set up on the covered treadle sewing machine, on a tree stand. We were dancing a fast schottische—all of a sudden over went the tree. Mom was so upset and mad. The dance was stopped and everyone helped pick up the trimmings. Since the holidays were about over, we threw the tree out. Mom got back into the holiday spirit and the dance continued. After that incident Papa always made sure the Christmas tree was safely fastened down.

One New Year's Day the old timers Ed McCann, John Hitz, Joe Chaney, Michael Sara, Sig Hopstad, and Uncle Reno visited from house to house, treating their friends to a drink from a big pot of "Moose-milk" egg nog to toast the New Year. Reno would clown around, dressed in his wife's squirrel skin parka, wishing everyone a Happy New Year. *Sis*

Dances

O h, the dances were so much fun! We always looked forward to them. They were held mostly during the Christmas holidays. Jim Downey, a sailor, and a friend named Jack O'Keefe, who stood about 6 feet 5 inches tall, came up on the steamship, "Tupper", from Seattle. Jim was a good accordion player and could play anything; a schottische, waltz, fox trot, Virginia reel, even a square dance. Both Jack and Jim liked Alaska and decided to stay. They fished, trapped and worked at the Nyac mine.

Our local boys could play good music, too. Andrew Miller, Raymond and Melvin Anderson, Henry Jung from Bethel, Moses Samuelson, James Kvamme, Joe and Elias Venes and Sam Samuelson played guitars or mandolins. Some of the men took up the violin. Noah Andrew from Tuluksak, who worked on a boat, was a fine guitar player. Also, Matfi Bereskin, who later became a Russian Orthodox Minister, played his steel guitar. Most of the dances were held at our house because we had the biggest living room. We also owned a large, great sounding console phonograph that filled the room with sound. Whenever the music would begin to slow down, someone would drop out of the dance and wind up the phonograph. Normally a good full wind would last one complete 78 rpm record. I remember inside the top cover was a picture of a dog and a large microphone; the RCA emblem.

Word traveled to Bethel and other villages about our dances. Dog teams would arrive, bringing the Hately family, Chris Nerby's, Oscar Hall's or our neighbors from Akiachak—the Harry Samuelson family. We were close friends of these people. They had kids our same age and we would be able to play with them for a couple of days. Jens Kvamme would dance the hambo. Ed McCann would dance the Irish jig or the highland fling. He taught me how to dance with him and I got to master that pretty well. Then someone would yell for the "broom dance" which is a fast dance. A single dancer would get the broom and slam it on the floor, and that meant everyone changed partners. Boy, what fun!

I remember one dance at our Uncle Reno's. We had no phonograph but there was a small Scotsman by the name of Scotty Morrison, who played

Moose milk, New Years Morning toast. Johnny Hitz, Lars Nelson, Ed McCann, Michael Sara, and Middy Chaney.

the fiddle. The men pushed the table aside for the dance. Two or three men grabbed Scotty and his fiddle, put him in a chair on top of the table and he was the musician for the evening. Sometimes dances were held at the bunkhouse. Johnny Hitz and Jay Cooke were staying there then. After our dances, they'd start frying up reindeer steak, studded with garlic slices, Everyone enjoyed them before going home for the evening.

It was hard to dance with some of those old timers. Johnny Hitz reeked of garlic. Sig Hopstad danced around and around until we would almost fall over. Some didn't know how to keep step. Others breathed too hard or had body odor. We'd try to get sympathy from our father, but he'd make us dance with them, telling us there weren't enough women to dance with and they wanted to dance. So, we accepted their dance requests and they went home happy. *Sis*

Communication

Sigurd Hopstad, a Swede, was the village ham operator. His call letters were K7COF. He reported weather conditions for air planes coming and going. He reported any emergencies and kept in communication with the doctor at the Bethel Hospital. Sig and his wife Katie had two children named Martha and Olaf. Martha was the oldest and met Jay Hagerty, married young and moved to Seattle, Washington. The Hopstads took in another girl, Katie's niece Florence, and raised her because her mother had passed away. Florence attended school with us in Akiak. The Hopstads moved to Bethel in about 1942.

Sig was a comical person. I can remember him dropping a coin and saying, as he picked his coin up "Yump! You-son-of-a-gun-Yump! How many times have I yumped for you!" Sig wasn't much on going outside during the winter to do chores. One day a friend went to visit him at his home and founding him sawing a log inside his house—feeding the wood stove right next to him. It was a comical situation.

Our folks ordered a Philco radio from Seattle and it came on the steamship. Each night at seven o'clock, all the old men from the village would come over to listen to the news. Some of the men would hold their heads very close to the radio because they were hard of hearing. While they listened, we were sent to our rooms to do homework and couldn't make a bit of noise. I remember hearing about Amelia Earheart making her flight around the world and about her being lost and never found. I remember Will Rogers and Wiley Post taking off from Fairbanks, in 1935, for the North Pole and crashing close to Point Barrow . Also, I remember hearing about the war breaking out in 1941 and about the Japanese bombing Pearl Harbor.

After the news, the men would light up their kerosene lanterns and go back to their respective homes. Then we were able to make all the noise we wanted.

In 1939, Admirals Byrd and Amundsen went on an Antarctic expedition to the South Pole and they needed all the best dogs from Alaska they could get. A boat came up the Kuskokwim River and stopped at Akiak and they took four of my grandfather Venes's best dogs, and some from Carl I. Carlson. I heard Colonel Norman Vaughn was on the same expedition.

Sis

Winter

S eems like the winters were colder then than they are today. The blizzards lasted a couple of days or so and we got a lot of snow. Each home had ventilators, a small hole covered with screen for fresh air, up close to the ceilings. They would be covered or closed when not needed. We could always tell how strong the wind blew outside by the sound coming from the ventilators. It whistled and the harder the wind blew, the more whistling we'd hear. We'd spend most of our time inside during a storm. After a big snowstorm, all of us kids would go outside with our shovels and make long, deep tunnels in the snow or make big snow men.

One winter, one of the pilots going to Nyac, the mine, had to stop at Akiak for a couple of days to weather out a storm. Clarence Marsh came over to see my father that night. Papa was outside doing some chores and when he came in Clarence asked him, "Arthur, what kind of weather is it out there?" Papa answered, "Cool and dark'n hell"—one of his favorite expressions.

Some of the radio operator's wives tried to answer the radio if their husbands weren't around. Sig Hopstad was gone at the time so Clarence Marsh went to see if Katie could get the Nyac weather report. They got Nyac on the radio okay, but, her son Olaf was laughing at her because she didn't know the first thing about radio operation. She quit in frustration. Clarence took over and got on the radio and it happened another wife was alone at Nyac, Elsie Pearson, wife of Fred Pearson the radio operator. Over the radio, Clarence asked her what the weather was like at Nyac. She answered, "clear and unlimited, foggy in the hills." Clarence Marsh laughed hard, it tickled him so much. He remarked, "What kind of a weather report is that?" He went down to the plane, warmed it up, and said he'd try his luck. He made it to Nyac okay. *Sis*

Floods

Spring arrived in April or May. The weather warmed up and the snow and ice began to melt on the river. The arrival of spring always energized us school kids—we got spring fever. The calls of geese, ducks, cranes, swans, and loons, filled the air. The swallows, robins, and chickadees chirped with happiness; everything came to life. May was the month the ice melted on the Kuskokwim, breaking up and moving out to Kuskokwim Bay. All of the villagers would gather on the bank to watch the ice crumble and begin to flow. It was a joyous event for the village. A large bonfire was built on the river's edge. The older boys

Flood—Papa and Willie in the Canoes with school house in the background.

brought their instruments for a songfest. We sang songs and delightfully toasted marshmallows over the open fire into the wee hours of the nights. Along the Kuskokwim, the winter nights are long, but beginning in early spring, we are blessed with nonstop daylight through July—one of the fortunes of living in Alaska.

Springtime always brought a threat of floods too. A large stick was carved from a willow branch and placed at the river's edge to monitor the water level. The marks on the stick were constantly checked to see if the water was rising or dropping. When the ice moved down the river on it's slow, steady pace, the water level remained constant and everything was okay. There was no threat of flooding then. Sometimes, though, the water would stop moving. This was usually caused by an ice jam downriver. The river's water level would rise fast and meant we had to prepare for flooding.

Most of the floods were quite small but occasionally we'd have a large one. When the water got too high, the villagers protected their furniture and miscellaneous possessions from water damage by stacking them on top sawhorses, stilts, carrying them upstairs or anything else they could think of. The animals were moved to higher ground inland or even placed on lower rooftops.

There were a few times when the water came into our house and we were forced to move to the upstairs of our home. Thank-goodness, the floods lasted only a few days and never caused extensive damage. We kids were in our glory when it flooded because school was cancelled. We'd spend our free time

Left—Gyda, Little Hans standing, and Melvin Anderson holding Dorothy.

paddling around in skiffs and canoes checking on our neighbors to see if anyone needed help. Occasionally, someone would fall overboard and needed to be quickly rescued. Luckily, there were no fatal accidents. The fun didn't last long, though, as the water soon receded. Afterwards, the work began. Everyone had to clean and scrub everything and put everything back in their rightful places.

When I recall spring along the Kuskokwim, my memories are joyful ones-filled with the excitement of singing, toasting marshmallows and cancelled school. *Sis*

Fishing

W e didn't go to fish camps like a lot of Eskimo people did, but did our fish cutting on the beach next to the river so we'd be close to the water to clean the fish. Papa made a couple of cutting tables, galvanized tubs were used for dis-cards and two large fish racks close by were used for hanging the fish. The slight breeze that came off the river helped to lightly dry the fish. Then the salmon was moved to the smoke houses where the fish was smoked with alder wood until completely dry and ready to eat.

The first fish of the season was smelt. We would go to Smelt Slough, 5 miles below Akiak, to dip for smelt. We only made this trip once each spring since the smelt run only lasts for a few days. We set up tents and cooked outdoors on a campfire. The boats were anchored next to the bank of the slough. We took turns standing in the boats and dipping for smelt with our long-handled dipnets. Sometimes, someone would fall over-board, net and all, and then be rescued by catching hold of their hair or suspenders. Finally, when the boat was full of fish, we'd take down our camp and return home where processing the fish began. There was always so much work stringing the smelts up to dry. It was usually the girls job to do the stringing. All dressed in kuspuks—an Eskimo windbreaker of cotton, which we could always wash easily, we'd sit around in a circle, on logs, stringing smelt on willows tied together to make a strand. Then the boys and men came along and hung them on a fish rack to dry. We girls would be so glad when this chore was done. It was such a smelly job and even after we washed our hands it took awhile to get rid of the smell. The smelts were tasty when dried and smoked but they were usually fed to the dogs for their winter food supply.

There was no limit on salmon then. We could go out and get as many as we could take care of in one day—cutting, drying, salting, and canning. King salmon was cut up for eating. Mom would put on her kuspuk and get out her well-sharpened ulu—a half-round Eskimo knife made of steel with wooden or bone handle. She would cut flat slabs from whole kings for eating, or make salmon strips to hang up to dry and then smoke. She

Barbara with her kuspuk on got out her well-sharpened ulu and cut flat slabs from whole kings

also used a special brine in which to soak the salmon before drying. She never allowed us girls to cut king salmon. She thought we would ruin them while cutting. She had her own way of preparing fish. Our job was cutting up pike or silver salmon for dog food. There was a cooking pot for the dogs, close to where we cut fish , and we kept dog food cooking with many scraps, as we split the fish, The dogs were tied up on the beach in the summer months close to the river. There was always a slight breeze to protect them from the mosquitos. The boys helped cut fish for dog food.

When we got older and were able to go fishing, my brother Butch, and my Uncle Elias, would take us girls along—mostly Ruby and I. Of course, we liked to go out in the boat on the water. The boys usually fished from a skiff with a 10 or 12 HP engine. When they strung the net out to drift, it was necessary to row to keep the net straight. Ruby and I would man the oars. We finally wised up to the boys. All they wanted us along for was to do the rowing. No wonder they were whispering and laughing, and acting as if something was amusing. We quit going because we got stuck with more than our share of the work. Finally they agreed to take turns with us.

There was also Pike Slough where lots of pike were caught. Mom cut them up to dry but Papa never cared for them. Besides being hard when dried, pike took up smoke house space. He'd say, "I don't know why you like them, they're just like chewing a piece of cardboard." They were, but

There was no limit on salmon. We could get as many as we could take care of in one day.

we girls thought them tasty. *Sis*

ℰntertainment

We got together and decided to put on a play. The only short plays were at Christmas school programs. One play stands out in my memory. Agnes Schlosser was the director. The name of the play was "Henry's Mail Order Bride" and it included a wedding. The background setting was the kitchen area with open cupboards and pots and pans hanging around. We found the perfect place in the bunkhouse. It had an open room, just right for seating at one end. Carl I. Carlson, the storekeeper, was the mail order bride. George Chaney, the best man, Catherine

Village play—Henry's Mail Order Wife—1940—Ruby Reno, Carl I., Catherine, Hanna, George, and Sis.

Kawagley was the bachelor and groom. My sister, Ruby, played the minister and my sister, Hanna, and I, were attendants. People from the surrounding villages came to see our play. It was humorous and entertaining and we were later complemented on our acting.

Ruby's father, Wilfred Reno, carved a wooden puppet. He called it his

Marionette; with strings attached. He'd put on shows with it. We liked that. His skill at making his puppet work for us made him very popular. He also played the violin and sang songs such as "I Wonder Who's Kissing Her Now?"

After the dinner meal at home, Hanna and I got to be the performers. We'd act out different people and their style of dancing—imitations of individuals with comical actions. Everyone would laugh so hard, as we did a pretty good imitation of people, I guess. It was funny and it became an evening ritual.

Ptarmigan hunters—Elias Venes, Harvey Samelson, Sonny, Johnny Dahl, George Chaney, and Joe Venes Jr.

Oscar Hall sold his store, 5 miles below Akiak, to Mr. Link, who was the U. S. Commissioner. They'd hold dances in the store. Papa would hitch up the dog team and we'd all go down. After the dances it wasn't so far to come home again.

Ben Kawagley, living on the other side of the river, would have dances once in awhile too. We'd all walk across the river in the winter, to attend the dances. Ben and Minnie's son, Carl, lived with his father. He was an older brother of the Kawagley children who lived on our side, and Carl was our friend, too. On the weekend, as we got older, we'd take off for Bethel to see a special movie or a dance, stopping at Akiachak where our friends, the Samuelsons lived. Their father had passed away and they owned a trading post. Their mother, Marie, ran the trading post after his death. Their kids would hitch up a team and head down to Bethel with us. Sometimes after the activities, we'd hitch up a dog team and start back home. It would be pretty cold at times, but we always dressed with parkies and mukluks. We carried a sleeping bag along for emergencies— in case someone got too cold. I fondly remember the cold, bright moonlight nights with the stars out. I can still hear the sled runners gliding over the snow through the wooded portages. *Sis*

Early Romances

W e started having boy friends in our teens. Hanna was older and already dating when Ruby and I got interested in boys. The boys we began to admire were boys from our village and the boys from Akiachak. The Samuelson boys were always around—Ted, Harvey, Sammy, and Bill. My brothers were interested in their sisters and cousins. The boys were nice looking and lively. Sammy was a good musician and could play the guitar real well.

Hanna, Ruby, and Sis breakfast at camp.

Ed McCann had a couple of boys named Jack and Harry, whom we called, Buggy. Also there was Albert and Jim Kvamme, Adam Kawagley and Pat Smith. At dances, we'd get romantic and sneak a kiss or two. Parents would always try to match us up, but it never turned out to be anything serious. I think it was because we were all close friends and since we were together a lot, we were more like family.

Ruby was the lucky one. She had a boyfriend that we girls envied. His name was Johnny Dull. He learned to fly and had an airplane, a J3 Cub. He'd come to Akiak from Bethel flying his airplane and would shower Ruby with expensive gifts—musical jewelry boxes, cosmetic kits, phonograph records, and boxed candy—things she liked. We girls were always envious but she wasn't serious about him. A few years later she met Emmett Shaw, from the Platinum mining camp. He came up to winter at Akiak with a family friend, Harry Wilson. Ruby and Emmett got married.

Papa had a mining partner by the name of Tom Secanoff, a husky

Russian everyone called "Pinky." With his squeaky voice he'd say " I come from McGrath, you know, with a couple of dogs, you know." Anyway, he took a liking to me and after Papa came home from a trip to Bethel, Pinky sent me boxes of candy. Papa would tease me. I liked the candy, but it got so I couldn't stand to even see Pinky.

Butch, Bessie, and Elias on a camping trip.

Soldier boys who were stationed at Bethel, would drive their jeeps over the frozen river to our dances. There were a lot of nice looking boys, but we were never allowed to get too friendly with them. The folks kept a good eye on us, while the soldiers were around. If we had to go to Bethel, even for just the dentist or doctor, we girls had to stay with Grandma Hall. She had girls herself so she kept us all in line, home at a certain time, and she got us up to go to church on a Sunday.

My Aunt Nora married Charles Guinn, who worked on the sternwheeler, after she came back from finishing high school at Eklutna and Mt. Edgecumbe. Charlie and Nora had moved into one of Chris Nerby's log houses when their first child, Susan, was born. I stayed with them for awhile. One night, I had a date with a boy named Ed, I can't recall his last name. He seemed like a nice boy. We went to a movie at the Northern Commercial store, the only theater in Bethel. A boardwalk stretched all the way down Front Street. After the movie, we walked back home over the boardwalk. It was a nice, cold moonlit evening. Just before I went into the house he kissed me. We had our arms around each other. It was then he needed to pass gas and the sound vibrated through the night. He then had the nerve to laugh. You might know, that ruined our romance. I was young and romantic and so humiliated. I never went with him again.

There was another romance that soured me. My sister, Hanna, met Ronald "Swede" Johnson, a bookkeeper and construction worker, who worked on the airport. They decided to get married and went to Fairbanks

Ruby, Hanna, Sis, and Carl I. camping out.

to live. Swede was called into the service so I went to Fairbanks to stay with her, and to attend high school. After school, I worked at the drugstore fountain. Sometimes I'd have to work until after dark and there was no bus service then. Some of the boys from home were in the service stationed in Fairbanks. When they had time off, they'd come visit at Swede and Hanna's house. If someone we knew was there, Hanna would send them after me to walk me home. Among the service friends were Roy and Clyde Hall, Fred and Amedee Chaney, and Jimmy Kvamme. One night, nobody came for me so our former teacher, Peggy Naas, who was our neighbor, sent her boarder down to escort me home. He was a soldier from Boston, Massachusetts. He had quite an eastern accent. It was a nice evening, cold with the moon shining. When we got home to our gate, he threw his arms around me and said, "The moon affects me so, I could crush you in my arms." Seems like I always wound up with oddball boyfriends. *Sis*

Bethel

The population of Bethel in the 1920s and 30s was about 400. Everyone knew each other. Each spring, as soon as the ice left the river, a steamship came from Seattle and then again in the fall before freeze-up. They brought food and building supplies or whatever was ordered by the settlers on the Kuskokwim River. Sternwheelers and private scows or barges would meet the ships from Seattle. As they were unloaded, the sternwheelers would haul the supplies to each village, delivering as far up the river as McGrath.

There was a complete boardwalk built on Front Street from the Moravian Mission across a swamp to Olson's Store and then to Brown's Slough. A small bridge was built over Brown's Slough where John Samuelson had a trading post and a few homes were built. Beyond, was a settlement called Louse Town. All of the businesses in Bethel were located along Front Street—the Moravian Mission, churches and the Northern Commercial Company which included, besides the store, a movie hall and a place for weekend dances. Also, there was the marshal's office and jail, magistrate's office; or commissioner's as it was called then, Louis Moncher's Store, the Post Office, Ole Hoffseth's Roadhouse and Restaurant, Territorial School, Bureau of Indian Affairs School and Offices, Chris Nerby's Store, a sawmill, and Olsen's Store.

Movies were never planned in advance. Whenever one was going to be shown, a kid would walk up and down the boardwalk ringing cow bells. He would be rewarded with a free movie ticket for his efforts. Sometimes older people would get the job. Mrs. Hofseth (Chigvick) was one of them. She had a bad leg and we all knew just who was ringing the bells, just by the sound of her gait on the boardwalk.

Fred Mock also lived on the boardwalk. He had a large house and would hold dances once in awhile. His live-in housekeeper, Martha Jordon, would play the music on her accordion.

Ed Stevenson, the fish commissioner, lived on the boardwalk, too. He had kids our age we'd play with and we like to go into their house, out of curiosity. We'd hear jokes about how, when you walked into his house, you wouldn't be able to stop until you hit the other end. Well, it wasn't that bad, but the house was built on permafrost and it made the foundation and floors shift, which made it awful crooked.

Our folks had a friend named Neil Corrigal. He had a boy, Robert and a girl Jenny. Jenny was our age and she'd want us to stay with them whenever we came down from Akiak. Their mother died when the children were quite young and Neil raised his kids himself. Oh, Neil was a great talker so it was hard to get away from him. He talked to anyone who would listen. Neil had a bad knee from arthritis. If you asked him how his knee was, he'd slap it so hard it would make you wince. He'd say "Bad, all I need is some Denver mud," which was used as a mud pack. I believe Colorado was his home state.

The "Greasy Spoon Cafe," a small shack made up as a hamburger and short order place, was run by an old gentleman, Orin Goodrich. He wasn't a very clean cook but I guess he made tasty hamburgers. We'd stop after a movie for pop or coffee as we liked to visit with his waiter, Jack Kennedy. Jack was a good storyteller and entertainer who had the appearance of a worn out range cowboy. He became our good friend. The river bank began to erode in the early 1940s and the boardwalk was dug up, so Orin bought another building further back and he named it "Dew Drop Inn." Jack went to another job of woodcutting. Orin took over Ole Hofseths live-in waitress named Martha Jordan. It was never as good as when Jack was there.

In 1933 the hospital at Akiak was torn down and rebuilt at Bethel. BIA figured it was a better location to serve the coastal area. The airlines moved in, construction started on an airfield and Bethel started building up. The population is about 6,000 now. *Sis*

Wedding

In the fall of 1941, Aunt Nora Venes and Charles Guinn met and decided to get married. He was working on the sternwheeler, Wallace Langley, that barged freight up and down the Kuskokwim during the summer months. The wedding was held in Bethel and an airplane brought them to Akiak for the wedding reception we were all prepared for. The reception was held at Carl I. Carlson's living room in back of the store. Eats were prepared and a dance was held. There was a wedding cake and nice gifts. We girls had practiced a song for weeks. With Gyda at the piano we sang this special wedding song, to the tune of "The quilting Party—On the

Charles Guinn and Nora Venes.

107

Kusko."

> In the sky the bright stars glittered
> On the shores of Akiak
> For it was there that Charlie's eye caught Nora's
> On the banks of Akiak
> Now he's seeing her forever
> She's his newly wedded bride
> Best of luck and our congratulations
> To the groom and for the bride

The older boys decided to play a few jokes on the newlyweds and while the reception was being held, they went over to the cabin where they were to spend their first night and hung tin cans under the bed springs. It was a fun wedding for our small community.

As the years have gone by, Nora and Charlie raised a large family and taught school in various villages. Nora became the magistrate at Bethel and then became the first Eskimo Judge of Alaska. They also were involved in retail stores for many years. *Sis*

Religion

Papa was Catholic so we were naturally baptized Catholic, also. Mama was Russian Orthodox. Fathers from Holy Cross Mission would come by dog team a couple times during the winter and by boat in summer. They would baptize newborns, perform marriages, or arrange for catechism studies and other duties. Father O'Connor baptized Hanna, Sonny, and me. My Godparents were Ellen Hall and Clarence Clark. Father Menager and Father Lorente were next and they baptized the younger children. Our household had the most children in the village and we were Catholic, so mass and prayer meetings were held in our home. Those priests were very enjoyable. They'd visit our school, tell stories, play the little organ we had, and lead us all in song. We liked to have them come. There wasn't much education in religion, aside from whomever was assigned to help teach catechism.

Saturday was our bath night, other days it was sponge baths. Our folks heated up water in a big copper kettle and we took turns bathing in a big aluminum tub. We were all clean for Sunday, a complete day of rest for us all. We had to dress nice and no work was done. We'd go visiting, play games and go on dog team rides. Sometimes Papa would bundle Mom and us all in a large basket sled and go for a long drive, or sometimes we'd go by ourselves. Sunday, us girls would have to take turns baking a cake or pies for the dinner desert. Middy was a good bake and he'd help us. Mom always made a special dinner for Sunday.

Sometimes we'd go across the river to the other side with Gyda or the Kawagley kids to visit the Moravian Church. We could hear the church bell ring about a half hour before the services. It gave us time to get over there. There was never any objection. When we asked Papa he'd say "Go ahead, why not, you know—after all there is only one God." The ministers

We had 12 good husky dogs and a large basket sled we used to travel from one village to the next, or to go on Sunday drives. We liked to ride around to see the country and visit friends.

were Reverend Trodahl, Schottsneider, Drebert, Dittmer, and sometimes Reverend Michael. They'd bring their wives occasionally. There were quite a few Moravians on our side too, so the ministers were glad to visit our community. We were happy to see them, too. We knew them well and enjoyed them. *Sis*

Disasters

In the early spring we'd go to the surrounding lakes to hunt muskrat, geese, and ducks. The older boys went hunting one day and weren't gone very long before they returned all excited. Andrew Miller's gun had accidentally gone off and shot Uncle Joe in the leg. The boys carried him home and called Dr. Myers from the other side. He came over, treated and bandaged Joe up. He had to be off his feet, in bed, until he could get around with crutches. Andrew felt so bad about the accident, he'd spend his time singing and playing his guitar for Joe while he recuperated.

Fred and Elsie Pearson moved from Nyac to Akiak. She was a daughter of another large family, George Hoffman of Napiamute, located above Aniak. They had one son, Fred Jr. who attended school in Akiak. Elsie had one bad leg and walked with a limp. One day she had a doctor's appointment at Bethel, so she asked Henry Jung to take her there. Henry had his own sled and dog team and agreed to take her down to Bethel. While going down the Akiak hill, over the sled went, turning Elsie upside down. She hit her head on a log and cracked her skull open. Sig Hopstad had to radio for a plane to come get her. She stayed a long time in the hospital recovering.

There was a shooting one night. I was pretty young then and don't know the exact details. Two brothers, Carl and Tom Madsen, came to visit their sister, Minnie, who lived at the end of the village. Alcohol was involved. There was a big argument and a fight between the brothers. Carl shot Tom to death. I can remember Marshall Anderson coming from Bethel and taking Carl away.

Every disaster occurring made an impact in our community. Alfred Anderson's wife, Elizabeth, got sick. Her boys were off at school and Alfred was spending a lot of time at their Canyon Creek mine. She spent too much time alone and just went off the deep end. Alfred was called home and the family had to take her out to the insane asylum in Seattle, Washington. Alfred Anderson's family then moved to Washington, the same year his brother, Ole moved his family to Vashon Island, Washington. A year later Carl I. Carlson sold his business and, with his niece, Gyda, moved away to Vashon Island. One by one people slowly started moving away.

My grandfather Venes passed away in 1938. We didn't know too much about cancer then, but I'm sure that was the cause of his death. Joe Chaney went to the Mayo Clinic in Minnesota to check a sore on his lip, where he held his pipe. It wouldn't heal. The Mayo trip didn't cure him. He died at the Bethel hospital of cancer. Afterwards Uncle Reno came down with cancer and he passed away at the Anchorage hospital. It was a sad time for the village and for our family. *Sis*

Alcohol

The miners always had their drinks. A home brew barrel was made way before Christmas. Other families did the same. When liquor got in short supply, the men would hire Uncle Joe with his fast team to make a trip to Bethel, over the tundra. Driving time to Bethel was two hours, or four for the round trip. Chris Nerby, a good friend, had a grocery and liquor store in Bethel. Chris would fill out the order, help Joe load the sled, and send him back to Akiak. The men could set their time by him. They'd be watching for Joe to come across from the portage on the other side. The dogs would start barking and across the river he'd come, stopping right between the houses.

No one seemed to get too much out of hand at the dances, because everyone was too busy dancing. A few occasions, the Chaney boys would have a fight and go rolling around outside in the snow. The older men would advise "let them go at it, they can't hurt each other." Sure enough, they'd be back dancing with everyone, everything forgotten.

One day, Hanna, Ruby, and I, went to visit the Kawagley girls, Catherine and Alice. There was a large drainage ditch with a board bridge we had to cross. We passed by Lars Nelson's house, Ante and Karen's, Pete Sara's, and Joe Chaney's, enroute to Minnie Kawagley's home. Coming back we saw this man laying still under the bridge. We got scared, thinking something terrible had happened. We ran into the first house, which was the bunk house, to report what we had seen. A few of the men went to investigate and found "Red Bean" passed out. They picked him up and brought him home to bed. I never knew his real name. There were always those nicknames that stuck. Anyway, he was short, fat and had red hair—an exact "Red Bean."

One cold winter morning, there was great excitement on both sides of the river. Ben Kawagley had lost his little boy, David, about 3 years of age. The day before, Ben hitched up his dog team, dressed David warm with a parkie and mukluks, put him in the sled and went to Bethel. Ben got drunk and on his way home the sled turned over and he lost his boy on the trail. Ben didn't realize it until the next morning. Immediately radio communications were made between the villages of Bethel, Akiachak and Akiak. It seemed another team from Akiachak was not too far behind Ben, fortunately. That dog team driver picked up the boy and brought David to his own home in Akiachak. He couldn't figure out who the child belonged to, but reported it. Ben immediately went down to Akiachak to claim his son. I'm sure it put a big scare into Ben! *Sis*

Changes

arl I. Carlson wanted to retire so he sold his store to the Laplanders in 1941 and moved to Vashon, Washington. Per Spein put his son-in-law, Tim Twitchell, in charge of the trading post. His wife, Annie, was the daughter of Jens Kvamme's wife. Twitchell's had four children at the time. I worked for them helping in the house with the children and washing diapers by hand. Since Mrs. Carlson had died there, Annie always said the place was haunted. One night, one of the kids got sick and Tim and Annie had to take her by boat to the doctor in Bethel. I had to stay alone with the other kids. It was a windy night and I was scared. The place was cracking and groaning. I took the three little ones and moved them into the Twitchell's large bed. I climbed into the middle and put the covers over our heads. We survived the night but I was afraid of staying there another night alone.

Grandma Smith and Patrick moved to Bethel. Patrick joined the Army and went to school. Grandma Smith moved in with Dad Brown at Bethel. Everyone called him "Dad." We didn't know his real name. He was the father of the bush pilot Nat Brown, and Lew Brown, whom Emily Smith married. Later when Grandma Smith would reminisce about that period in time she'd say, "Well, when I was living, I mean when I was cooking for old Dad Brown—" We'd all laugh. We knew she was living with him. After Dad Brown died, she moved up to Nyac.

After that, the miners never came to Akiak to winter over. Instead, they went to the lower forty-eight to winter or else stayed at the mine. A school opened in Nyac. Pauline Chaney taught BIA school for a year or so at Tuluksak. They now had a family of their own, so they moved to Nyac, where their kids could go to the Nyac school with other children, and Willie had his work. The other older boys and girls joined the service or left for jobs they found elsewhere.

We, who were left at Akiak, tried to liven up the place. We made Grandma Smith's vacant house into a dance hall and called it "Moose Hall." Moses Samuelson came up from Bethel. He and Uncle Elias would take out their instruments and play for the dances. The younger folks from the other side came over to join in for a good time, but it was never the same again. In the meantime, Papa got a generator, so we had electric lights. It was such an improvement over what we were used to. *Sis*

Butter and Egg Man

William Pete, a trader from Aniak, drove his truck over the ice to Bethel. He was one of the first to drive from Aniak to Bethel. He hauled freight for his store. A close friend of the family, Evelyn Hall or "Auntie" as we called her, tacked the name "The Butter and Egg Man" on Willie. He'd stop at Kalskag to pick up his friend, Paul Kameroff, to travel with him. Willie called Paul "the Reverend." Willie and Paul were friends of Tim Twitchell's. They would always stay at the Twitchell's a day or so to visit. One fall, they were traveling a little too late and got frozen with their boat and freight, so they had to remain in Akiak until the ice got strong.

For entertainment, they'd join us kids on our skating parties. They were both good skaters and we enjoyed having them. When the ice got strong enough to walk on Paul and Willie decided to skate to Bethel, because they wanted to get home to their families. Bethel is about 40 miles from Akiak. They skated to Akiachak and stayed overnight at Marie Samuelson Forrest's trading post and the next day arrived in Bethel. They got a plane to fly them up to Aniak. Later that winter Willie came down to get his boat and freight.

Jack Kennedy, another good friend of ours, bought out Andy Smith's trading post at Tuluksak. Jack was an old cowboy from Texas, we got acquainted with him while he was a waiter at the "Greasy Spoon Cafe" in Bethel. He had an appearance of being on the range too long but he had a wonderful personality. He was very gracious, played the harmonica for the dances, was a good storyteller and was ever so lively. We all loved

Jack. We'd see him coming way up the river, traveling with three or four dogs pulling his sled. The kids would run to greet him and escort him to Akiak. Jack's business didn't pan out, so he got Middy Chaney as a helper and they cut wood and sold it to earn money. After a year or so he moved to McGrath where he spent his last years. *Sis*

Willie, a likeable Eskimo business man, had a variety of customers because he could speak Eskimo as well as English. A story teller and entertainer, Willie would take out his guitar and sing the favorites of the time. One that was always a great request was called "Oh, Don't You Believe It." about a down and-out gold miner that came to Alaska but dug clear to China and found nothing but rock. He'd mispronounce his words while he sang or talked, it was comical but we knew what he meant. For an example I heard him speaking to his small grandchild, pointing to a helicopter, overhead. Do you see that? It's a Helencofter.

Willie and Cecelia had a large family, and in the early fifties, sold their store at Aniak and moved to Bethel and started another store, a few houses away from our home. Their younger girls, Margaret, Bertha, called Bing, and Linda became close friends with our girls, spending a lot of time between houses. Bing tells of the time she asked her Dad how to spell, Chicken. Her Dad said "D O G, spells Chicken." She believed him until she started school. Bing told her teacher that she could spell and her Daddy had taught her how. So she spelled chicken for her teacher. It didn't go over well with the teacher and she spelled chicken for Bing. Bing went home so put out at her father. Willie told Bing it was a big joke but from that time on the girls never asked him how to spell any words.

Fairbanks

Hanna met Ronald Johnson, we called him "Swede." He was a bookkeeper for the Northern Commercial Company and also took inventory for the Twitchell's Store. Catherine Kawagley met Clifford Anderson, who was working on the Bethel airport. Both Hanna and Catherine got married. Catherine moved to Bethel and Hanna moved to Fairbanks where Swede was called to go in the service. Swede was stationed at Galena so I went to Fairbanks to stay with Hanna. I flew up with Frank Barr, who became the mail carrier after he was hired by Gillam. Hanna was working at St. Joseph's Hospital and I got a job right away at the same place. Sister Solange was in charge of the kitchen and I worked under her. We became close to Sister. She was such a fine person and I can remember her and I gathering lots of nice vegetables to serve on the hospital menu. There was a large garden behind the kitchen.

My former teacher, Peggy Naas and her husband, John, lived across the street from us. I liked the telephone so much but didn't know many people in town. I'd call John on the phone just to be talking on it. 1 can't even remember what I talked about. I think I just rattled on just to be talking on a phone.

One day John Naas decided he'd take me downtown to show me Fairbanks. Clyde Hall was there at the time and decided to come with us. Now, Fairbanks had a red light district on Fourth Street in those days . John walked me right down in front of the houses, little log houses, all in a row. All of a sudden, Clyde made an excuse to meet someone and took off in another direction. John and I continued walking right down in front of these houses, John was tipping his hat to the ladies and making small conversation. I petted all of the little Pekinese dogs that they all seemed to have and we continued downtown. It was later I found out why Clyde made the sudden disappearance. He remarked, "I wouldn't be caught dead being seen around there and in broad daylight, too."

Sundays, we liked to ride around to see the country and one day the Naas' asked Hanna and me to go riding with them. We drove on these rolling hills to Ester Creek, an old mining settlement, and visited their old friends, the Leonard Seppala's. They knew them from the Nome area. Leonard Seppala was the famous musher that made the diphtheria serum run with his dog team from Fairbanks to Nome in the 1930s. They had a nice retirement log home with a beautiful flower garden. We had an enjoyable day with them.

We lived about a mile from downtown on Second Street. I quit working to attend Lathrop High School, the only high school in Fairbanks then. Art Johnson's family lived across on Third Avenue, and a block down the street lived the Albert Hagberg family. The kids were my age so we'd run through people's yards—any short cuts to get to school. When the temperatures were forty to sixty below, no one seemed to mind and we were never stopped. We became close to the Johnson's and Hagbergs. They reminded us of our own folks at home. So we'd have family gatherings and the mothers would take us all to church on Sundays. The Johnson's had four boys and a girl. All the boys were airplane minded— working summers for Wien Airlines and all eventually became pilots. All died in airplane crashes. The two oldest Hagberg boys are gone and now we're left with lots of good memories

One cold winter day, on our way home from school, one of my girlfriends and I stopped at Star Cab to warm up. That is where I first met Robert Lindsey. I liked him right away. We got to know each other and he'd give me a ride to school or take me home after. With those bitter Fairbanks temperatures, his rides were a real welcome. We never went on many dates except for an occasional movie.

Hanna had a baby boy on the 28th of December 1943, and named him Harvey Arthur. Swede transferred back to Fairbanks and in the early spring I went back home to Akiak. Bob wrote me a few lines that spring and said he was called into the service, so we lost track of each other for awhile. *Sis*

Cannery

hen I got back to Akiak, most of the older boys had gone into the service. The Kvamme boys, Chaney boys, and the Bethel boys, were all stationed at Fairbanks. Uncle Joe Venes and Sonny were stationed at Fort Richardson in Anchorage. I stayed for awhile in Akiak until early summer when Helen Sara, Ruby and I decided we'd like to go to Bristol Bay cannery located at Clark's Point. Since we weren't eighteen yet, we needed a guardian. So, Helen's father, Mike Sara decided to take us under his wing since he was going to fish there. We flew over to Clark's Point Cannery in Bristol Bay. My job was putting lids for the cans into a machine and sealing them, after the can was filled with fish, before processing. I worked there until I was asked to work in the kitchen, setting and waiting on tables at the mess hall. After the cannery closed in late fall and the main crew left, we continued to work as a cleanup staff. We went to Dillingham by boat and took Nicholson's Air Service to Anchorage. Elmer Nicholson and his brother Herb were pilots. The Alaska born Nicholson brothers were good pilots, having the reputation of knowing the western coastal area of Alaska better than any other pilots. Elmer flew us over to Anchorage.

I put an ad in the Anchorage paper to be a home helper for my room and board as I wanted to go back to school. It was answered by the Harry Baker family. They owned Yellow Cab at the time and had four children, who all attended school. So, I became their companion. Harry and Peggy Baker were busy with their cab stand. My brother, Sonny, was at Ft. Richardson so he came to see me. He told me he met someone in his troop that knew me from Fairbanks and his name was Robert Lindsey. Bob and I started dating again. I stayed about 4 months with the Baker's until Ruby and I got a place of our own. Then Bob decided to propose to me.

One evening we went to a show on base and that night he proposed to me and presented me with an engagement ring. He had just received his transfer papers and was leaving for California, and then to an overseas base. We were married at the courthouse in Anchorage. Since I was almost 18, I needed someone I knew well to give me away. An old friend, Otto Thiele, gave me away and Ruby stood up for me. Also, a few close friends were present. We were given a surprise wedding party afterwards. Marie Forrest, from Akiachak, was in town then. I was so glad to have an old family friend at the wedding. Our wedding night was spent at the Lane Hotel on Third Avenue. A few days after, Bob was on his way to Bakersfield, California—close to where his folks lived at Jackson, California.

California

Bob made arraignments for me to come down to California. I left with another army wife and her baby, from Elmendorf Air Force Base. It took us close to 12 hours on a DC-3, stopping only at Annette Island. The weather was bad and we had to wait there for a few hours. When we got to Boeing Field in Seattle, we stayed at the Richmond Hotel. The poor baby was very tired from all the traveling. Early the next day, we parted company and I left by bus for California. I can remember stopping at a small stop called "Weed" just below the Oregon border. We took a bus break at an old western type building. I was so thrilled as I had read about that place in one of the old western books by Tom Mix.

Bob met me at Stockton and we drove to Jackson, California, where I met and stayed with his folks. He stayed a couple of months at Bakersfield, California and then was transferred to Ft. Benning, Georgia and then on to Panama, which was considered overseas. After he left, my sister-in-law, Juanita, and I got a job working in Stockton at a POW camp. The camp held German prisoners, who packed and shipped tools to American stations overseas. It was a well organized camp and we worked right along with the prisoners. During the time we worked there, President Roosevelt died. I remember how we stopped for a minute, in silence and prayer, in remembrance of him. President Roosevelt was a great president and it was a tragedy to lose him, especially while we were still at war.

Bob's folks moved to Tracy, California so Juanita and I quit our jobs and went along with them. Bob's father, Glen, was hauling fruit across the country. While we were in Tracy, my brother Sonny was being transferred overseas and visited me there. We had a great time sightseeing, Three days later he left for India. It was the last time I saw him.

The summer was so hot and I was subject to nosebleeds so I arranged to go up to Vashon, Washington to visit my friends Carl I. Carlson and his niece Gyda. I liked it up there and of course, saw a lot of mutual Alaska friends. I picked fruits in the fall. There were crops to pick: berries, apricots, peaches and apples to make extra money. In the winter, I worked for an egg processing plant, candeling and sorting eggs.

I was getting ready to join Bob in Panama after he found an apartment for us, but, his dad died in California so he came home for the funeral. Since he had only a short time left overseas, he decided to stay in the states. I went to California to join him. He was to report to Ft. Lewis, Washington. Bob had bought a Chevrolet coupe. We loaded everything we possibly could into this small car and drove up to Washington. On our way up the highway, on the pavement, was the biggest snake I've ever seen. Bob and I stopped and looked at it—from inside the car. I had seen a lot of smaller garter snakes in Washington but never one as large as this. I wondered whether it would be safer to run into a large snake in Washington—or a bear in Alaska.

Arriving at Ft. Lewis, Washington, we got a nice apartment and I met and became friends with several military wives. We were still at Ft. Lewis when the war was declared over and all the overseas troops started coming home to America. My brother, Sonny, was stationed in Calcutta, India and then Karachi, Pakistan. Some of his battalion came home by boat but, he was in an Army transport plane. His plane caught fire and crashed into the Gulf of Salerno, Italy. There were seven survivors, but all the rest perished—the majority of the passengers were, and, still are entombed in the plane at the bottom of the ocean, including my brother. The survivors had parachuted in time, but a few other parachutes didn't open soon enough. Their bodies were picked up; otherwise only debris came to the surface.

I decided to come home to the folks and, since I was expecting my first baby, decided to stay with them until Bob got out of the service, which would be in the early spring. I took the Alaska steamship, S. S. Alaska, out of Seattle to Seward. It was pretty rough on the sea and I was seasick most of the way. We made stops at Juneau, Wrangell, Sitka, and Valdez. It was good to be able to get off ship and visit the towns. My first grade teacher, Blanche Sullivan, lived in Valdez and I got to visit with her, too. The trip to Seward took 3 days. After arriving at Seward, I took the Alaska Railroad to Anchorage, then took a Pan Am flight to Bethel and a bush plane to Akiak. It was so good to be back home. I had not realized how much I'd missed the folks. It was such a blow for them to lose Sonny. I am sure by my coming home, it helped to lift their burden. Cutie and Charlie were home too. Bess was going to high school in Bethel. Butch and Elias were in the service yet and Grandma Venes was home.

The year was 1946 when I traveled on the Alaska Steamship passenger ship to Seward. Earlier that spring, in March, the S. S. Yukon went on the rocks on the southeastern route. There were eleven casualties. The rest of the passengers were safely evacuated. This was the last year of the Alaska Steamship passenger trips to Alaska.

While I was outside my friend, Helen Sara, met Acey Neimeyer down around the cannery. She married him and moved to the lower 48. Berntina Kvamme married Tim Twitchell's brother Ben and moved to Takotna. Alice Kawagley met Boyce Osterhouse from Dillingham. Together, they moved to Dillingham. *Sis*

The Gold Dredge at Nyak.

Home Again

When Tim Twitchell's family left Akiak and moved to Takotna, Alaska, Clarence and Bergie Marsh bought the Trading Post. Their daughter May Lou was still with them. They had two other children, Clarence Jr. or "Sonny" as we called him and Dorothy. Sonny was

Platinum mining Camp near Good News Bay

The old Platinum Mining Camp near Goodnews Bay.

taking flying lessons elsewhere and Dorothy was in Bethel going to high school.

Ruby was home with the folks. Her husband Emmett was working at the Goodnews Bay Mining camp named Platinum. She was waiting on her first baby and would be closer to the hospital in Bethel. Uncle Joe Venes, Jr. met a girl while in the Alaska scouts at Nome. Her name was Helen Simon, After he was discharged from service, he went back to Nome and brought Helen to Nyac, where he was working. They got married and she later moved to Akiak to stay with Annun, my grandmother, while waiting for her first baby.

Ruby was the first to have her baby. It happened during the night. She

Nyac—1950. We spent two happy summers and a winter at Nyac.

had it earlier than what was predicted. Mom helped deliver Ruby's baby boy named Wilfred, or Billy, as we called him, in January of 1947. I was pregnant at the time too. Because Ruby gave birth at home, I was a bit frightened to be so far from a hospital. Mom insisted I take the first plane to Bethel so that I could be near the hospital. I was very happy to go. First I stayed with Nora and Charlie, then with Hanna, who moved from Fairbanks to Bethel at the time. It was a miserable, cold winter that year with so many blizzards. It was a blizzardy night when I had to go to the hospital to give birth to Aimee Lee. Bob had been transferred to Fairbanks for the duration of his service time, so I sent a telegram to tell him about our beautiful little daughter.

I went back to Akiak after Aimee was born. I couldn't find any diapers anywhere in Bethel, so went to Shorty Moncher's store and bought a bolt of flannel. Mom and I made a bunch of diapers on her treadle sewing machine. Those were the best diapers. I used them on a few of my other babies also. Helen Venes got to the hospital okay and she gave birth to a baby boy named Joe Jr. on April 1, and it wasn't an April Fool's joke either.

The Marshes, who owned the trading post in Akiak stayed until early spring of 1947. The trading post business was slow for them. Clarence would go off for a day or so looking for another way of making a living, leaving Bergie and Mary Lou, to tend the store. They'd come over in the evenings and we'd play games for entertainment, and they'd wind up spending the nights with us. Bergie constantly complained of the noises and spooks at the old store. Our folks had a lot of room and we enjoyed the company. There wasn't a school on our side of the river anymore, so Bergie ordered a correspondence course for the three that needed it—

Mary Lou, Lena (Cutie), my youngest sister and brother Charlie. She taught them every day from the Calvert Course, besides taking care of the store.

In March, Clarence and Bergie decided to move to Bethel and go into the restaurant business, taking Mary Lou and Cutie to finish the school year in Bethel. That left me to help

Robert (Bob) Lindsey and Sis.

Charlie finish his school course. The next school year, Charlie went to the boarding school at Holy Cross Mission on the Yukon River. The school was run by Jesuit priests, and nuns were the teachers. Charlie was way ahead of his class. Bergie and I were very happy to hear that, as we had put a lot of effort into their correspondence courses.

The last traders at the old store at Akiak were Charles and Hattie Hoffman. Hattie was a childhood friend. Her father, Tom Conquest, was a store owner who had bought Mr. Olson's store along side of Brown Slough at Bethel. Charlie was the son of George Hoffman, another old timer with a trading post and a large family at Napaimute, close to Aniak. Charlie and Hattie had quite a few kids. Shortly thereafter Swede and Hanna bought Per Spein's house and moved to Akiak. The village was lively with children again. The Johnsons had three or four kids, too. But after a couple of years the kids were getting bigger so Charlie and Hattie decided to move back to Bethel to enroll their kids at school. Business was pretty slow at Akiak. Eventually Swede had to go off to find work. Later Hanna and the kids moved to Bethel to join Swede and so the kids could get an education.

Bob was discharged from the Army in April and came to Akiak, but only for a short time. He had found a job at Platinum And I and the baby followed him. We had a nice house at the camp. Ed Olson was the boss. It was a well organized camp with lots of nice people. Ruby and Emmett were there, as our neighbors, and also our good friend Harry Wilson. For entertainment, there was a movie once a week. When Bob got off work in the evening, we'd take out our fishing poles. Bob rigged up a baby pack for Aimee and off we's go over the hills. There were several fish-laden

Sis and the Lindsey kids—Renee, Aimee, Robert, Bruce, and Barbara.

trout streams and we always caught enough for a good fish feed.

In late fall and freeze-up, the Platinum mine and camp closed for the winter so we moved to Bethel, renting one of Shorty Moncher's rental houses. Early the next spring Bob got an offer to go to work at the Nyac mine. Knowing most of the miners and men from Akiak would be there, we were anxious to go. Especially since living quarters were also provided. My father was working at the mine as was Ole Anderson, Joe Venes and his family, Blackie Peltola, Buck Arnold, Clarence Clark, and Willie and Middy Chaney and families.

It was a nice camp with young workers from Akiak, Bethel, and Aniak. The bosses were J. K. Crowdy and Bill Race. The camp cook was Jerry Frankie and laundry workers were Ellen Hall and Alice Samuelson Jones. Alice met a miner named Joe Mendola and later got married. We spent two happy summers and a winter at Nyac. Bob bought a small cub plane. After work we'd take our two kids Aimee and Renee and fly around the area.

The Nyac camp celebrated the Fourth of July. There were a lot of children with games, prizes and plenty of food. Everyone had so much fun. On Halloween, we had a masquerade party and dance. The best costumes were awarded prizes. The prizes were gold nuggets and were awarded by size—according to first, second, and third place. We made a trip to Akiak with our plane to visit the folks and spend Christmas with them. Yes, our lives at the camp were full of activity. We were happy and content.

The following winter we decided to go back to Bethel. Bob was

Bob Lindsay and Jimmy Hoffman, our mailman, with their Norsman.

interested in flying. We rented Neil Corrigal's house right across the street from Jack Peck. Jack was a pilot and instructor. Jimmy Hoffman and Bob took up flying, which included the written material, with Jack as their teacher. After they completed the written instruction phase, they went on to Fairbanks for their flight training. They successfully completed flight training. Bob was pleased and I was proud of him.

Charlie and Aunt Nora Guinn had bought Olson's store from Tom Conquest, who also had a few other buildings for sale. When Bob completed his flight training, we decided to buy one of the buildings and remodel it into a home. We moved it up alongside Brown Slough, close to the water's edge, so we could fish conveniently and have a place to dock a boat with a motor. My brother, Butch, who was home from the service at the time, joined Papa to help Bob build a second story on the house. We needed more room. Our family was growing with five little ones—Aimee, Renee, Barbara, Robert, and Bruce.

Bob worked for awhile for Ray Peterson's Flying Service. Later the business changed over to Northern Consolidated Airlines. After a couple of years, Bob went to work for Alaska Airlines as a pilot, also. Flying the passenger and mail run were: Ray Miller, Sonny Marsh, Art Johnson, and Sig Krogstad. My sister, Bess, was the secretary and radio operator. My

Ruby and Billy—Sis and Aimee—1947 at Platinum.

brother Butch was one of the ground crew and Wally Johnson was the airplane mechanic.

In April of 1954, Bob and Wally, while flying a Norseman to Platinum on a mail run, ran into a "whiteout" on the way back to Bethel. They crashed and burned at Jacksmith Bay. They were killed instantly. It was such a hard time for me, left alone with our five

children—Aimee, Renee, Barbara, Robert, and Bruce—all so young! I was so thankful I had my parents. They came right down from Akiak to stay and help me with the kids until I was under control again.

I was working at the post office then. Ethel Schmidt was the post mistress. She suggested I come back to work as soon as I was able, which I did. She said it would keep my mind occupied, but I can remember sorting and bagging mail with tears streaming down my face. I know there was a lot of wet mail sent off. My biggest worry was my little ones. As it went, with the help of family and good friends, I got through it all.

Bob was a member of the Alaska National Guard and also the newly formed V.F.W. Post which he helped build at Bethel. We were all honored by the members of the V.F.W. dedicating the Post to Bob: The Robert V. Lindsey Post 10041. *Sis*

Changes

I'd always had girls from the villages whom I hired to stay in our home and help with the children while I worked. It seems I went through a lot of them. Some girls, who were extra good, I'd try to keep. Some of them were dandy breadmakers. In those days, you couldn't go to the store to buy a loaf of bread, so they were virtually forced to learn how to bake. I tried to hire the ones who were especially clean and good with the children. Of course, some weren't very competent. I remember one who even had a case of athlete's foot whom we got rid of in a hurry. In those days most young families had girls who came in to help in the homes while mothers worked.

My sister, Bess, worked as secretary and radio operator at Alaska Airlines. She met Charles Matthews, who was stationed with the Air Force at Bethel, and he was being transferred to another base. Later, in 1955, she quit her job when she and Charlie decided to get married. I quit work at the Post Office and decided to try Bess's former job at the airlines. I didn't stay with that job very long. I just didn't like all the paper work.

I spent some time at home. One morning, Bergie Marsh called me. She said one of her cooks had not shown up and she needed someone to give her a hand with the cooking, and could I come? That was the start of my cooking career.

Roy Troseth came to Bethel in 1955 and I was introduced to him by Hanna's husband, Swede Johnson. They were on the same job at the Bethel airport. We took a liking to each other and he made me happy again. In the winter of 1956, we decided to get married. We were married in Fairbanks on 17 March of that year, making Bethel our home. Roy Jr.

and Chris were born while we lived in Bethel.

In the spring of 1958 disaster struck. I had never seen my father sick before so it came as a great shock when he suffered a massive stroke and passed away. Such a great loss for all of us and especially for our mother. She was left alone at Akiak. A couple of years later, Butch fired up his cat and sled and, along with other family members, moved her house to down the river, over the ice, and placed it near his home Bethel. There she spent her last years.

Roy and I moved to Anchorage in the fall of 1959—renting out our home in Bethel. Roy worked on bridges up and down the highway and on to the oil platforms. At first we rented a log home in Mountain View, which is still in use today. Then we bought a home on Diamond Boulevard, close to where the Diamond Mall is located. Aimee went to Wendler Jr. High, the younger ones at Abbot Loop Elementary. The elementary school was close to our home. In the summer of 1961, Roy had a job at Manley Hot Springs, building a new bridge there. As soon as school was out for the summer, the kids and I drove up and stayed with him. It was a fun time. The kids could go fishing when they wanted and every evening we'd all go swimming at the hot springs. When the job was almost over and most of the crew had left, I was asked to cook for the remainder of the crew. That fall we decided to move back to Bethel, renting out our Anchorage home.

Back in Bethel, Roy decided to try the restaurant business. We rented a place and called it the "Kusko-Queen." He ran it for over a year but then tired of it all. It just didn't pan out for him. It turned out to be too much effort for too little pay. Roy gave it up and went back to construction. In the following years, Erik and then Gordon were born. Both Roy and I were very saddened to learn that Gordon was diagnosed as having Downs-Syndrome. Renee went to Copper Valley Boarding school in the fall of 1963 and Aimee went there in the fall of 1964.

Roy was back in Anchorage working on the Matanuska Valley bridges when the earthquake struck in 1964. The kids and I were still living in Bethel. Our home in Anchorage was badly damaged with a crack from one end of the house to the other. The people who were renting fled, leaving the house as it was. The neighbors had to push the doors open to get them out. The TV turned over on the floor and all the plumbing was damaged. The toilet turned over and there was a lot of damage to the pipes. Roy had to redo just about everything to make it livable again. The renters never came back for their belongings and we heard that they left the state.

Roy suggested we move back to Anchorage. We figured it would be better for the family, and, there would be more opportunities for Gordon. In those days there was no schooling nor training for the handicapped in Bethel. We left Bethel and moved back to Anchorage. Robert remained in Bethel to finish high school. He stayed with his Uncle Butch and his family. After graduation, he joined the service and served in Vietnam

In the summer in Anchorage, I worked at Emard's Cannery at the dock downtown. In the fall I started working at the Woodhaven Rest Home and did so until they closed. Not far from our home, a new rest home was built named Ridgeview Manor. Roy Johnston was the supervisor and Dorothy Eaton was the head nurse. One fall morning, after the older kids had gone to school, I heard a knock on the door. It was Dorothy Eaton running in to say they needed a cook at the Ridgeview home as the cook called in sick and they couldn't find anyone to help. She knew I had the younger ones at home, with no baby-sitter, and suggested I go cook for the day and she'd take care of the little ones. The patients had to eat so I went down and made the meals for the day. That day was quite interesting. What other place but Alaska can something like that happen? I continued cooking at Ridgeview Manor for a while. Sis

Bruce's Hunting

In Anchorage, after the great quake, Bruce was big enough to enjoy hunting. When the birds started flying in the early spring, he'd get the urge to take his .22 rifle and go hunting. Bruce had figured out just how to bird hunt in Anchorage. In those early years, the city of Anchorage did not stretch out very far. Dimond Boulevard was still unpaved and considered an isolated area. Since Bruce didn't drive yet, he'd ask me to take him to his favorite secluded hunting spot in an area which is now Dimond mall. He'd get me up at three in the morning and I'd drop him off, and return for him in a couple of hours. It was always so quiet with everyone asleep. When we'd return, Bruce would be so happy with his catch. Other times he'd go to a lake within walking distance from our house and would leave early in the morning. One day, he came back with a couple of nice fat geese. He complained about having to shoot one nine times before he finally hit it. A few days later, a neighbor lady came by and asked us if we had seen a tame goose of hers that had been missing for a few days. We told her no, we didn't know there were any tame ones in the neighborhood. Discussing it later, we recalled that the one I'd cleaned had a different type of breast bone than the others, and that solved the case of the missing goose. *Sis*

Goat

One day, Roy brought home a baby goat given to him by a friend in Eagle River. Oh, the kids were so happy. It was so playful with them. I even liked it. But, as it got older, it became a nuisance and I was constantly chasing the goat out of the house with my broom. When the neighbors complained that it would eat the clothes off their lines, we tried penning it up, but, "Billy" the goat always seemed to get out. One day while getting ready for John's birthday party, I made a beautifully decorated birthday cake and put it on the table. Kids began arriving for the party and the goat came running in with them and jumped right up on the table and started eating the birthday cake—with me and my broom after him. That did it for me and the goat! The next day, we returned him to the original owners. Sis

Seward

In the course of time, John and Arne were born in Anchorage. In the summer of 1968, Roy came home from another job. One day that summer, we decided to make a picnic lunch and take the kids on an outing. It was a beautiful June day and the Marathon Run was taking place in Seward. Coming home late that night, we found our house burned. The inside was gutted out and we were left with nothing. Worst of all, we lost our dog in the fire. We were all so sad and full of tears. I remember sitting on the outside step, crying, wondering just what was going to happen to us. Thank-

Roy and Sis on their 25th wedding anniversary.

fully, we were pretty well known around the neighborhood and the neighbors all came to our rescue. We received many donations of food, clothing and cash to help us out. Later, we found out it had been an electrical fire. We stayed with my sister, Hanna and with other friends until we were able to find an apartment to rent. *Sis*

Valdez

In late 1968, Roy left for a job in Valdez. We were unhappy apartment-living, so he decided we should try Valdez since it looked like it might be a long job for him. We found a place and tried living down there. It was a great opportunity for Gordon. Previously, while living in Anchorage, we had taken him for training at the Alaska Crippled Children's Association. When we moved to Valdez, we were able to enroll him in a newly built Alaska Retarded Children's Association Complex. It was called the Harborview Memorial Hospital. It had a hospital at one side of the complex and a home and school for retarded children on the other side. We enrolled Gordon right away for schooling. Roy and I were thrilled to have Gordon in such a fine facility. There he received excellent training to become semi-self sufficient. It eased my mind to know he was getting proper help.

In Valdez, Roy was usually working out of town on construction jobs or doing some work around town and was kept very busy. The boys always wanted me to drive them to a hunting or fishing area. I took them on weekends, or on early afternoons after we had finished our household chore. One weekend the boys wanted me to take them to some well-stocked streams they knew of around Glennallen, which lies beyond Thompson Pass. Packing a big picnic lunch, fishing poles, and a .22 rifle—just in case we needed it—I got the little kids ready and off for the day we went.

Driving over Thompson Pass, we saw many ptarmigan. Roy Jr., Chris, and, Erik, were just learning how to handle a gun and hunt. They were so excited to see all the ptarmigan and wanted to try their luck at shooting.

143

Since Bruce was their instructor, a conversation took place, as I listened. "Come on Bruce, let's have Mom stop so we can shoot ptarmigan. They'd be so easy to get." Bruce answers "No, we're not hunting any ptarmigan. They're breeding and having babies. Just how would you feel if someone shot you while you were breeding?" No one said a word, including me. I just drove along in silent humor toward a good fishing stream.

We tried living in Valdez for a year. It was a while before the pipeline was in operation, but construction had already begun. Roy worked on the dock unloading pipe for the pipeline. Later he was called to different parts of Alaska for bridge work again. We didn't care for living in Valdez. The weather annoyed us. When it rained it never seemed to stop. When it snowed it was the same story, so we decided to move back to Anchorage. Gordon remained at the Harborview Hospital, staying for schooling and training. *Sis*

Wasilla

In 1970, Wasilla was still a small place. Jim Kennedy, at one time, owned quite a bit of property around the area with his home in the middle of Wasilla. Jim liked our family and encouraged us to buy him out. Jim was 90 years old and he wanted to get rid of the house and acreage. He offered us a good deal and we accepted it.

We had quite a time cleaning up Jim's place. He was a junk collector. When we finally got it cleaned up, we planted potato patches and got chicken and pigs. In the years we have been in Wasilla, we've had horses and raised a few calves. Our place is a typical small farm. It's right in the middle of Wasilla, too.

The old Kennedy house in Wasilla.

Jim was a short, stocky, hard working man, gun collector and forever buying, selling and trading. Everyone liked and respected Jim. He loved to talk and tell stories, graciously speaking to ladies with "Yes Mum." Jim spoke of his early days and of being a horse rustler in

Montana before coming to Alaska. He had been a blacksmith and rode in Buffalo Bill's Rodeo when he was young. While reminiscing, he'd take a box of Copenhagen snuff from the breast pocket of his hickory shirt, pound the top hard with his fingers, open the box and take a pinch of snoose, repeat the same process and return the box to it's special place. He said he'd chewed all his life and when he passed on he was taking this box with him.

In the early days, Jim always had home brew cooking in his basement.

He told us humorously how he rigged up a small barrel under his wife, Jessie's, rocking chair. Jessie would sit and visit with friends rocking and talking and never realizing she was encouraging his brewing process. We never knew his wife. She died at an old age, before we met Jim.

Jim had a small trailer house and

Wasilla home.

lived by us the first summer. We all became attached to Jim and he liked the kids. We started taking care of him and inviting him to eat with us. He had a habit of sleeping with a pistol under his pillow, and a rifle by his bedside, after he once had a bad experience with a break-in during the night.

Early one morning, I ran over to Jim's trailer to check on him before starting my morning chores. I raised my head and was face to face with the biggest moose I've ever seen. I screamed loudly, turned around and ran back into the house. The startled moose ran the other way. I was watchful after that. Moose were all around in Wasilla then.

Jim had a German Shepherd dog which he said was always getting mixed up with porcupines. The dog would come home loaded with porcupine quills. It was a hard process to remove the quills with no vet close by . The only way he could take the quills out was by hanging the dog upside down until the dog passed out. Then he'd pull the quills out of the dog's mouth. He got rid of the dog because the dog couldn't learn to stay away from porcupines.

Jim met a lady, who was in her late fifties. He wanted to make a trip

146

over the highway and he asked her to do the driving. Together they loaded the trailer and made the trip okay. He came back in early spring and announced that they had gotten married. Jim had bought a home at Anchorage in Mountain View and they moved in. She had an ex-husband that was living in Anchorage. She began seeing him again and both started taking advantage of Jim and his

The Troseth boys: Erik, Roy, John, Arne, and Chris.

finances. Before long, Jim was taking care of them both. Jim got mad when he realized what was going on, so he loaded up his trailer and moved back to Wasilla. That was the end of that marriage. He left her the house and property in Mountain View. Jim rented a small house on Lake Lucille at Wasilla until he moved into the Pioneer Home in Palmer. He died at the age of 100, with his snoose in his pocket just like he wanted. He also boasted that his long life was credited to having one short glass of whiskey in the morning and one before retiring at night.

We had a horse named Tony. Roy was raised around

Sis' grandson, Jason Anvil and a mess of berries. Berry picking was a family event. We'd even have berry picking contests. We knew Papa would win because he was left-handed and could pick with both hands. I have a daughter, Barbara, who has inherited his style of berry picking. Anyway, at the end of the day, we'd all climb back into our boat and head for home. Everyone was tired but we had all of our buckets full of berries, ready to clean and store away or eat. The salmonberries and blueberries were used in various ways, mainly for jams, jellies, pies, Eskimo ice cream (agootuk), or as a desert with sugar and cream.

horses as he was growing up and he wanted the kids to learn how to ride and take care of horses. Tony was feisty and wasn't easy to ride. The kids were afraid of him. He'd buck them off once in a while when he didn't want to be ridden. Roy was the only one who knew how to handle the horse. One Fourth of July, after our big day at the VFW festivities, Roy was feeling no pain because he'd had a snort or two. Wearing the large cowboy hat he wore all the time, he harnessed and saddled Tony and rode out of sight. About three o'clock in the morning I woke up and Roy hadn't come home yet. I looked out the window and couldn't see the horse or Roy anywhere.

Chief Wasilla's corner—a buying trip to the village.

Just then, around the corner they came, looking as if they'd been on the range for a awful long time. It was a sight to behold. It seemed like a real chore for the horse to move his legs and Roy riding and hanging on the saddle, like he was almost asleep. I sure wish I had a camera then as it was very amusing. I went back to bed and the next day I heard Roy had ridden the horse right inside all bars in Wasilla! He and the horse were treated like royalty, which was very obvious.

We had a pig named Petunia and we bought her because she was a runt and we felt sorry for her. She remained a runt for a long time then she finally started growing. Petunia became quite a pet— running in and out of the house and playing with the kids. One day, while in the garden, I was called into the house to meet a visitor. I dropped everything and went to the house with Petunia close at my heels. My visitor was a well dressed insurance salesman. Petunia began running and squealing around his legs. I finally chased Petunia out with my faithful broom. The poor man was so startled, I will never forget the expression on his face. We agreed to sell Petunia when she got bigger. She was too much of a pet for us to slaughter.

Henri, the calf, was small when we got him. We always seem to get to attached to our animals, and since our porch was low on the old house, Henri would try to come into the house. My friend from Anchorage, Henrietta Hansen, came up on the train to stay over night. We called her "Henri" also. She didn't know we had a calf named Henri. In the early morning, I got up and took care of breakfast, Henrietta was still asleep on the couch. Henri, the calf, seeing the door open, came in and I began yelling and grabbed the broom to get him out. Henrietta woke up wondering what was going on. She heard me yelling, "Henri, Get out!" She thought I was yelling at her. She wondered why I was ordering her to get out. What a laugh we had when she realized I was talking to our calf named "Henri"

Roy worked on the city dock in Anchorage and one day had an accident. One of the operators of a crane dropped a beam. Roy was under it but saw it coming, he jumped backwards and landed in the water. He wound up in the hospital with a broken leg and nerve damage. He was unable to work again. We bought a large farm house and had it moved from Palmer to Wasilla, where we now live. We had rented out our old Kennedy house and one morning awoke to another fire. Jim's old home burned to the ground.

Sis' gift shop, Chief Wasilla's Corner crafts.

I took a job working as cook for the new Iditarod School and worked about 4 years, and then decided I'd like to try to start my own business. The Wasilla museum wanted to start a gift shop so I opened one up there calling it Chief Wasilla's Corner. I knew a lot of Native people from around the Bethel area and could get Native crafts. It was interesting and fun doing what I liked to do. But, after a couple years, I decided to buy a small building and move it close to my home. I did a lot of vendor sales between Fairbanks and Anchorage at festivals. But, that got old. The travel was too much wear and tear on my products and it got too expensive. Roy and I were having our problems, as he took to drinking too much and life became miserable. So, I sold the shop. I got a divorce and moved back to Bethel, working at the Phillips Alcohol Treatment Center as a cook. I remained there until Roy passed away in 1989 and then came back to our home in Wasilla.

Despite the sadness, we all went through—in the past year losing my

Arne Troseth on the Kennedy farm with Petunia the pig, and chicken.

son, John, and a couple of months later losing my Mom, age 90, we really have had a lot of happiness and can laugh over many comical things that have happened over our lifetime. So very many treasured memories to cherish. *Sis*

Auntie Ev

This book would not be complete without mentioning Auntie Ev. She was an important part of our lives in our later years. Evelyn (Hall) Ewald, a daughter of Oscar Hall, was a close friend of the Laraux family and was part of our lives, since she spent so much time with us. Evelyn attended the University of Alaska, then came back to her home in Bethel to work at the Northern Commercial Company Store. She met a serviceman, Paul Ewald, stationed at Bethel with the Alaska Communication System. His nickname was "Screwdriver." They decided to get married and after a month or so he was transferred to Anchorage and a year later to the lower 48. Ev went along with him from base to base until he was transferred overseas to Germany. When he left for Germany, he said he intended to send for Ev after he found a place for them. It never happened, though. She never heard from him again.

Autie Ev loved animals and children.

Screwdriver's family told her after a few months he had found a German girl. It was confirmed when divorce papers were served to her later.

Auntie Ev, as we called her, made her way back to Alaska and home to Bethel, where she started working as a cook on the river boats on the Kuskokwim River. During the winters she'd come to Anchorage and

151

Wasilla to stay until work started up again. When she got tired of my family, she'd visit Hanna at Clam Gulch, Alaska. We were always glad to see her. I was usually working and she was a big help to me. She loved children, not only mine, but all children. The little ones called her "Auntie Elephant." She got a charge out of it, as they all liked her. Money didn't mean much to her. With her paycheck, she'd buy the kids candy, ice cream, pop or anything she thought or felt they might want. Also, Ev was a religious lady and donated lots to the Catholic church. She enjoyed her liquor, but drank privately from a hidden flask she usually carried in her purse. But, she never got abusive and always controlled her drinking in a rightful mind.

Auntie Ev was a great entertainer, a wonderful storyteller of the days gone by and would imitate the old characters we knew as we were growing up. She passed away a few years ago, never to be forgotten. *Sis*

Our Family and Friends Today

T here are not many people living from the days of "old Akiak" except for our dear friend Minnie Kawagley Brink. She now resides at the Pioneer Home in Palmer, at the age of 98. We can count or name with our ten fingers just about everyone else our age that is still living, besides our family. Time has a way of just passing too quickly.

Hanna and Swede got a divorce after having four boys and two girls. Hanna remarried and now lives with her husband, Leonard Stormo. They own a lodge at Clam Gulch called the "Que-ana" meaning "Thank-You" in Eskimo.

Bess, Butch, Cutie, Sis, Mom, and Ruby.

Alfred (Butch) married a nurse, Marilyn Lesway, who was working at the Bethel Hospital. They were married and he went into the freight barging business on the Kuskokwim River. In the spring of 1980, while preparing his barges for the summer season and welding

153

a barge, an explosion killed him instantly. He left his wife, four boys and a girl. A few months later a similar accident killed his son, Paul. Marilyn still lives in Bethel.

Bess now lives in Wichita Falls, Texas. Being a military wife, she has gone from station to station with Charlie Matthews. They have three boys.

Ruby and Emmett Shaw retired to Moose Lake, Minnesota. They have two girls and three boys.

Lena (Cutie) married Glenn Gregory—a pilot and mechanic she met

Papa's fish cache.

while he was working for Northern Consolidated Airlines in Bethel. They lived in Fairbanks and then moved to Tanana, Alaska. They went into the trading post business and Glenn also operated a flying service. They retired and are now living in Fairbanks. They have seven girls and one boy.

Charles lives with his wife, Annie, in Enumclaw, Washington. He is a captain for Delta Airlines, has two girls by a previous marriage and he and Annie have a boy.

Uncle Joe was injured in a car accident in 1978 in Bethel. He died leaving a wife, Helen, and seven children. Helen has since passed away.

Aunt Nora and Uncle Elias live in Bethel with their families. Elias is the only one that eventually married a childhood sweetheart, Berntina Kvamme Twitchell. Both spouses were deceased and they got reacquainted and are living happily forever after. Elias has 10 girls by his first marriage, adopted a boy and raised his first wife's nephew.

I live in Wasilla and have had 11 children—three girls and eight boys. Seven are living at either Anchorage or Wasilla, three live in Bethel, my

Per Spein's old house.

son John is deceased. I am the grandmother of 25 grandchildren and five great-grandchildren and still may have more to look forward to.

I make my constant visits to Bethel for fishing season, berry picking and to visit my three Lindsey children, who have settled with their families there. Robert has the old family home and Bruce and Barbara are in Bethel, also. They take me by river boat to "Old Akiak." There they have a cabin and they plant potatoes in our old garden spot. The earth is still good. The family burial grounds are behind "Old Akiak." There's a few old houses still standing plus a few caches. The trees and grass have grown tall. I sit and reminisce of bygone days. What a wonderful life

155

we've had—picturing things as they were then—beginning with dog teams, boats, antique airplanes, and now to cars, trucks, speedboats, snowmachines, and jets. Memories, all fond, of how we were raised on the Kuskokwim River, at "Old Akiak"—*our side of the river*.

Akiak Today

Michael Sara's old house.

The family garden—Beautiful.

Remains Joe Venes' old boat.

Bernie Kvamme's house as it is today.